OWN YOUR
PAST
CHANGE YOUR
FUTURE

For God gave us not a spirit of fearfulness;
but of power and love and discipline.
—2 TIMOTHY 1:7 ASV

OWN YOUR

PAST

CHANGE YOUR

FUTURE

A Not-So-Complicated Approach to Relationships,
Mental Health, and Wellness

DR. JOHN DELONY

RAMSEY
PRESS

Published by Ramsey Press, The Lampo Group, LLC
Franklin, Tennessee 37064

This publication is designed to provide accurate and authoritative information with regard to the subject matter covered. It is sold with the understanding that the publisher is not engaged in rendering financial, accounting, or other professional advice. If financial advice or other expert assistance is required, the services of a competent professional should be sought.

Scripture quotations are from the American Standard Version Bible. Public Domain.

The names and other identifying facts of individuals whose stories appear in this book have been changed to protect their privacy.

Editor: Jennifer Day
Cover Design: Chris Carrico and Gretchen Hyer
Photography: Seth Farmer
Interior Design: PerfecType, Nashville, TN

ISBN: 978-1-942121-62-6

Printed in the United States of America
22 23 24 25 26 WRZ 5 4 3 2 1

To Sheila.
You hold up my arms when I am weary. You bring me true joy and you have healed my heart—I love you. Here's to many more adventures.

To Hank and Josephine.
My love for you two has no end. It is my highest honor to be in the arena, covered by dust and sweat and blood, trying to do my part to make your world a little bit better. Every day I thank God that he picked me to be your dad. May we always remember to stay a bit wild.

CONTENTS

FOREWORD
BY DAVE RAMSEY

I am continually amazed at the human spirit. Our spirits are unbelievably tender, fragile, and can be scarred. At the same time, our spirits are unbelievably strong and resilient.

Over the last thirty years, I've walked with tens of thousands of individuals and families overcoming their financial stresses. I've found that money is just one way people experience stress. Many people are often overcoming all kinds of other life stresses all at the same time. And I'm always impressed with the power that folks can have in their lives when they *believe* they can change and *choose* to make their stresses and scars their strength.

If you're reading this book, you've experienced some sort of trauma in your life, and I'm not saying that because I'm judging you or because it's some prerequisite. It's because you're human! We've all been through something hard. We all have some sort of crazy in our family. (I like to joke that if you don't, then it just might be you!) We've all had lies told to us by well-meaning people or lies told about us by not-so-well-meaning people. And the list of hurts goes on and on. All of these things have damaged us in some way. Unfortunately, we can't change our past. But we *can* change our future.

Winston Churchill said, "Out of intense complexities, intense simplicities emerge." The hurt and hopelessness we carry from our past can be intensely complex. But from it, the intense simplicity of truth can emerge. And truth is powerful. It's intense enough to cut through the complex and simple enough to make things clear. In this book, Dr. John Delony introduces truth to the equation of our past traumas and gives us a simple, clear path forward. Through personal stories and research, he shows us how the intense simplicity of truth can transform our hurts to healing and our hopelessness to hopefulness.

If you're not familiar with Dr. Delony, you're in for a treat. The first time I met Dr. Delony, I was immediately taken aback by his quick wit, authenticity, and unbelievable intellect. As we've worked together several years and have become friends, my respect for him has grown. His compassion and genuineness as he reaches into peoples' lives and helps them are astounding.

As you read these pages, you'll experience that same compassion, authenticity, and wit. You'll laugh. You'll cry. Your thoughts and actions will be challenged. And if you take the steps Dr. Delony outlines, you will be transformed. He will help you apply truth and hope to your life stories and write new ones—better ones.

The incredible thing about your stories is that, as long as you're breathing, your stories are being written. The question is: Who's doing the writing? Dr. Delony will give you the framework to help you pick up the pen and take the writer's seat. He'll help you put pen to paper, so to speak, and author new stories for your life that aren't warped by pain or disappointment or manipulation. You'll be able to move forward and live out new stories based on the truth of who you are and who you want to be.

So often we hear the phrase "controlling the narrative" and we immediately think of manipulative politicians or media. Don't be confused. That's not what owning your stories and writing new ones is about. It's not some public relations skill. It's about being honest with yourself and doing the emotional, physical, relational, and spiritual work that only you can do. It's about taking control of all-things you for the sake of you. It's about the legacy you want to leave. It won't be easy, but it will be worth it.

I'm excited for what will happen as you own your past and change your future!

ACKNOWLEDGMENTS

Few things are more challenging or humbling than getting a book out into the world. Truth be told, I would not have made it had it not been for the many dedicated souls who scratched, clawed, sacrificed, and dragged me and this manuscript across the finish line. I am forever grateful to everyone who climbed in the ring with me on this one.

Sheila: You lost me for the better part of a year while I completed this project. I am so grateful to you for picking up all of the early mornings, late nights, and lonely weekends while I wrote, rewrote, and rewrote yet again. You kept our home afloat, while also completing your own major projects. None of this happens without you.

Hank and Josephine: You two inspire everything I do. You had absent mornings, boring evenings, and even more boring weekends while I finished this project. I am back and ready for more adventures.

Dave Ramsey: Thank you for your trust, your wisdom, and the man you are behind closed doors. You took a risk on some no-name kid from a university classroom, and you have changed my life. You are the consummate coach and guide, always learning and pushing us to do the same. Thank you.

Cody Bennett: You are the perfect coach, support, and friend. You hold me accountable, you advocate for truth, and you are always in my corner. Most importantly, you have continued to live out these ideals with your friends and family. You are walking the walk and it makes me better. Thank you.

Rachel Sims and Eva Daniel: So much of what is in this book came from our brainstorming sessions, your prodding, pushing, and editing, talks we gave across the country, and y'all listening to me run my mouth for hours on end. You two are world class at crafting ideas, challenging me, and getting the best out of me. Thank you.

Preston Cannon: You are the best book publisher in the world. You are an even more incredible man, husband, and father. I can be a handful and you have worked magic wrangling me and getting this book across the finish line. Thank you for never giving up on me.

Jennifer Day: This book does not exist without you. Period. You are the best supporter, counselor, editor, friend, and writer anyone could hope for. You never let me settle, you challenged me to cut thousands (and thousands) of words so the reader wouldn't drown. You pushed me, picked me up, said no, and you championed this project from start to finish. You are one in a million—and I'm grateful I had the chance to work with you.

Kris Bearss, Rachel Knapp, Sam O'Neil, and Rick Prall: Thank you for lending this project your copyediting skills, your insights, your draft reviews, and the hours of citations.

Seth Farmer, Brad Dennison, Chris Carrico, Connor Bowser, Will Smith, and Brad (Natalie) Imburgia: Thank you for lending your artistic talents and for making the book look and feel right. You guys are wizards.

Wade Wilson and Tracy Pearl, Dr. Kristen Clark, Drs. Steve and Lynn Jennings, Dr. Michael Gomez, Todd Whitaker, Melissa Whitaker, Jon King, Jennifer King, Larissa Cable, Trevor Moore, Matt Foster, Randal Dement, Dr. Steve Bonner, Dr. Andy Young, Dr. Jeff Smith, Dr. Bret Hendricks, Dr. aretha marbley, Dr. Loretta Bradley, and Dr. Ian Lertora, Bob, Mikee, Brother, and Sister Delony: Thank you for your wisdom, for debating, reviewing, and reading, for arguing ideas, and for your insights and friendship.

Cory Mabry, Zach Ford, Caroline Slemp, Megan McConnell, Joanna Gaston, Amy McCollom, Caitlin Radecki, and Jasmine Cannady: Thank you for your marketing, writing, publicity, and project management brilliance.

Luke LeFevre: Thank you for the breakfasts, wisdom, and friendship.

James Childs and Kelly Daniel: Thank you for road testing this material with me for a few hundred shows. I am so, so grateful to you both.

Jeremy Breland, Suzanne Simms, Amy Severson, Jen Sievertsen, Blake Thompson, and the rest of the Operating Board: Thank you for the opportunity to write this book, your input on various drafts, and your leadership. Here we go . . .

• PART 1 •

The Stories Are
the Problem

CHAPTER 1

When Things Fall Apart

I quietly slipped out of my bedroom, careful not to wake my wife or young son. I grabbed a cheap plastic flashlight from the kitchen and silently undid the deadbolt on the back door. Wearing only my boxer briefs, I stepped outside into the backyard. It was pitch black as I waved the faint light back and forth in the rain to try and help my eyes focus.

We were coming out of the hottest Texas summer on record and clawing our way out of a devastating, statewide drought. There was a historical loss of agriculture and farming, and many of the lakes were holes of clay and dust. Everywhere I went, all anyone was talking about was the heat and how bad we needed rain.

Secretly, I was the only guy in the state praying for it to *not* rain. I know—selfish and lame. Of course I didn't want the drought to continue, but I couldn't afford to have my house collapse down around me either.

I probably should have led with this: I was certain my new house was falling down.

Shortly after my wife, infant son, and I moved into our new home, I began to notice cracks in the Sheetrock walls, spidering cracks above the doors, and tiny concrete cracks in the foundation. You had to look close to see them, but if you knew where to look, they were everywhere. I figured if it started raining, the sudden shift in soil moisture could split the foundation of my home, pour in through the cracks, and wreck me financially.

For years I'd been jolting awake in the middle of the night, never sleeping uninterrupted for more than a few hours. I was exhausted but used to it—this was just life. So on this particular night, it wasn't a surprise when my eyes popped open at 3:00 a.m., my heart pounding in my chest. But I *was* surprised to hear the water banging the roof and windows: the rain was here.

I stutter-stepped through the darkness on my toes, making my way to the side of the house. When I'd almost reached the far corner, I dropped down onto my hands and knees behind the cheap suburban boxwoods framing the flowerbeds. I shoved the flashlight in my mouth and crawled the rest of the way on all fours through the mulch, weeds, and mud.

My head near the ground, I was tracing the line where the concrete foundation met the flowerbed. Inch by inch, I crawled through the rain and dirt, looking for any sort of cracks in the slab and anywhere the water could be pouring into the house.

We had moved into this beautiful red-brick ranch home about a year before. It was the quintessential suburban track home in a new development where many of our friends lived. The country was still re-learning how to breathe following the 2009 economic collapse, and I had been nervous to buy anything. But my wife fell in love with this house, and I believed my family deserved a home. So we bought it, and I promised myself I would try and love it too.

Shortly after moving in, I began to notice the cracks.

It started when I noticed little splinter cracks around the doors and windows. I could see grout chipping away in the kitchen and paint flaking off in the living room. Then I spotted what looked like fractures in the foundation. In a few places, the concrete itself had tiny hairline cracks, and the exterior corners were beginning to crumble.

I was filled with rage. We'd just bought the house and it wasn't even ten years old yet! *Why hadn't the previous owner disclosed the issue? How had the inspector missed such an important problem? How had I missed it?*

My wife didn't think this was a big deal. In fact, she said she didn't really see the cracks, even though I repeatedly pointed them out to her. It was maddening. So I went to the internet, where I learned dozens of explanations and theories. Maybe the cracks were from the dry, shrinking clay soil; poor craftsmanship on the foundation slab; or cheap 2x4s milled from new forests. According to a number of different websites, my house was a disaster. The internet would tell me anything I wanted to hear.

Over the course of a few months, I invited several different buddies over. I'd show them around and point out every crack. There. And there. And over here. They would always mumble something about "settling is normal, man" or "your house looks really great."

I called different contractors out. They would show up with a mustache, dip cup, and an extended-cab truck. They'd walk around, measure things, and sigh heavily. But they found nothing. They all gave the house a clean bill of health. One told me to call back in a few years.

The contractors wouldn't take my money.

They were idiots. Incompetent. Liars.

Or maybe they felt sorry for me. After all, I was a young husband and father who had been suckered into buying a broken-down house. I was an embarrassment. Maybe they just didn't have the heart to tell me.

Finally, I called Todd, one of my best friends in the world. His dad was an architect, and Todd had grown up on construction sites. I was confident he'd know what I was talking about. He loaded up his family and drove three hours in the nightmarish heat to come check out my house.

I walked him around the house and out to the driveway. He listened quietly and soaked up my rambling explanations. After a while he turned, looked at me, and spoke directly and firmly—as only a good friend can.

"Delony, your house is good. It's strong. What you're seeing is cosmetic. The cracks are completely normal and there's not even that many," he said. "Dude, this conversation is over."

I was deflated yet resolute. I trusted my friend but I also knew that even the smartest people could be wrong sometimes. I could *see* the cracks in my house and no amount of disbelief from experts or friends or my wife could convince me that I wasn't seeing what I knew I was seeing.

Problem was, I wasn't just seeing cracks at my house. I was starting to see cracks everywhere.

Coming Unhinged

Outside of the problems with my house, my life was a chaotic blur.

I was a human hurricane, held together by a dress shirt and tie.

I was a senior student affairs administrator at a remarkable little university. One of my roles was leading the housing department, which meant I was responsible for the dorms—millions of dollars, countless employees, and thousands of college students. Every year, parents dropped off their kids on campus, and it was me and my team's job to take care of them. We taught them how to get along with strangers, how to turn the corner into adulthood, and we worked hard to create community and a home away from home. We were good at it.

But when thousands of young adults from all over the country move away from everything and everyone they know, and all pile into giant brick residence halls together, things get messy. When they did, I was often the guy who got called.

Students got wasted and ended up in the hospital. There were drugs and fights. Sickness. Attempted suicides. Car wrecks. Failing grades. Getting kicked off the team. Rape and sexual assault. Students or their parents passing away. Massive, paralyzing amounts of debt.

These kinds of challenges don't have office hours, and neither did I. My job never ended. I lived on a merry-go-round.

When the ambulance showed up, when someone needed to call Mom and Dad to let them know their child was hurting, in jail, or in a psychiatric ward, I was often the guy to make that call.

I was the guy people wanted around when the wheels were falling off. And I liked being that guy. I liked being in the know, and I liked figuring out ways to point people to the help they needed.

I was both good at my job and pretty arrogant about how good I was. I loved speeding through town at all hours of the night. I was honored to meet with police officers for drug searches and talk with hospital staff in the wee hours of the morning. I was gifted at sitting with hurting people and walking them through their darkest moments. Then I would roll out of bed the next morning, check my phone, squeeze in a workout, and start all over again.

In my day job, I was the one bringing the chaos. It was always budgets or personnel issues or student concerns or yet another board meeting.

I felt like my head was on fire.[1]

I said yes to everyone and everything.

Want to go to a leadership program at Harvard? Yes.

Can you leave your brother's wedding early to deal with a student death? On it.

Who can lead this new department? I'm your guy.

Can you teach one more graduate course? Done.

Interested in a second PhD? Absolutely.

Want to present your research at professional and academic conferences? For sure.

Texting, more texting, emails, clicking, notifications. Grade the papers. Write the papers. Pick up diapers. Keep moving. Keep fighting. Run, run, run. Do it all. And it was *a lot*.

I was married to a brilliant professor and scholar. She did her best to both live life with me and strategically avoid me. I was like living with a taser. After years of struggling with infertility, we finally had a new baby and we were trying to figure out how to be happy. We were juggling kid and careers, not sleeping, and setting up childcare—all while trying to be present for each other. And by "we" I mean "her." Sheila did most of the juggling. I was just plowing ahead.

Around this time I was also done with my faith. I didn't really believe in God anymore, and I was through with any sort of organized religion. But I worked at a faith-based university, so belief and organized religion were part of the job. I was trying my best to muscle through the motions in order to keep my job, my wife, and

---

1. During the writing of this book, I sent a draft to a few old friends who were with me during this part of my life. One of the guys, my great friend Kevin, told me that he got goosebumps when he read this line. He said he distinctly remembers me sitting with him and a group of other guys one morning, more than twelve years ago, and telling the group that I felt like my head was on fire. I do not remember the conversation or ever saying that, but I find it fascinating that more than a decade later I used the same exact words to describe the chaos in my heart, mind, soul, and body.

my community. Every day, I put my head down to grind it out, often struggling to believe the words that were coming out of my mouth.

I was a fake. A charlatan.

Oh yeah, and my physical body? From the outside, I was in great shape. I ran, lifted, supplemented, and tried every diet under the sun. Vegetarian. Raw vegan. Keto. Only protein shakes. Super high fat. Fasting. Atkins. You name it, I dragged my poor wife through it.[2] I was never consistent, always believing I just needed the one magic program or diet or combination. I'd often end up mainlining a box of cereal and a bag of gummy candies, only to declare that *tomorrow* I'd find the right new plan! I'd spend ten days on a new program, quit, and move on to the next.

And like I mentioned before, I didn't sleep very much. More accurately, I couldn't.

Years prior, I'd started taking sleep meds after my mixed martial arts training sessions went late into the night. I could train until 10:00 p.m., get home, take a pill, and slip out of consciousness with very little effort. But being unconscious is different than restorative sleep. Way different. So after years of pushing my body to the edge and then chemically knocking myself out and pretending it was sleep, my body had started to eat itself.

But I kept getting promoted, and I kept getting more responsibilities. I kept getting recognized. For the most part, I was pulling off my attempt at living a frenetic, nonstop life.

---

2. My wife was such a trooper. Eventually she just began asking me at the beginning of every month, "What are we this month?" I'd throw out some random fad diet, and she'd head to the grocery store and try to make it work. Or sometimes I'd offer to go to the store and I'd end up with a shopping cart full of barely edible nonsense. Like noodles made from fish hair or hamburgers made from Scottish goats with hyphenated names that slept in monasteries with late-century monks. Or gummy candies. I often got off the rails and just bought a clinically insane amount of gummy candies.

Or I thought I was.

This is right around the time I started noticing the cracks in the foundation of our home. I was noticing cracks in the walls and foundations of my friends' homes. And in the buildings at work. And in my faith heritage. And in my marriage. And in the economy, higher education, politics—everywhere.

I became obsessed with cracks. They haunted me. Nobody else wanted to acknowledge them, so I felt it was up to me to figure them out. And I *needed* to figure them out.

The more I looked for cracks, the more I found them.

And this is how I ended up in the middle of the night, soaking wet, crawling around in muddy flower beds in my underwear, looking for the water seeping into the foundation of my home.

Except . . .

There was no seeping. No leaking. I was on my hands and knees and I couldn't find water rushing into the cracks. There were cracks, but they weren't what I thought they were.

My house wasn't falling apart.

I was.

I'll never forget sitting down in the mud that night and taking the flashlight out of my mouth. I blinked my eyes for a moment, trying to clear the rain that was dripping from my eyelashes.

I started to laugh. And then I started to cry. I was laughing and crying at the same time. I was so exhausted, and so tired of being tired.

As the guy who got called when people were melting down in the middle of the night, it was not lost on me that, in that moment, someone might have called me about *me*.[3]

---

3. Yes, the irony . . . cue Alanis Morissette.

For a brief second, I worried that my neighbors might be watching. Or that my wife might be wondering where I was. I was always looking to see who was watching, like I was living my life on a theater stage.

But nobody saw me. Nobody was watching. My wife was sound asleep.

I was alone.

And as the guy who had a PhD, a highly visible leadership role, a young family, and all the answers to everything, I found myself in a scary place.

I knew I wasn't well. I wasn't having a psychotic break—far from it—but I couldn't keep going like this. I had lots of friends and people who I trusted, but I had no idea what to do next. I was sitting frozen in the eye of a hurricane of my own making.

When You Suspect It Might Be You

I know your life is different than mine. We look different, think different, have different experiences, and have different opinions. But as the great theologian and writer Frederick Buechner once said, "The story of one of us is the story of us all." My story is your story, and your story is my story. We are bound together.

Maybe you've never worked for a university, you're not married, or you don't have friends who tell you the truth. Maybe you're rich or poor. Maybe you have a law degree or maybe you dropped out of high school. You're a democrat or a republican or a pacifist or a multi-tour veteran. You may be black or brown or white, seventh generation or a recent arrival. Maybe you're twenty-four or maybe you're sixty-four.

My story is your story and your story is my story.

And everyone is struggling.

I've spent the past two decades researching, teaching, and serving thousands of people in different capacities. I co-host a nationally syndicated radio show and my own caller-driven podcast. I speak to thousands of live-event audience members across the country, and my family and I are involved in our local community. I'm hearing it from all angles.

Our lives have been turned upside down. Everyone is struggling.

You are trying to make your marriage work, trying to hold things together during the pandemic, trying to make sense of wild economic news or fires or someone you love passing away. Someone labeled you with anxiety or diagnosed your kid with autism. The bank foreclosed on your house. You're angry all the time. People treat you as less-than because of how you look. You don't believe in your work anymore. You were horrifically abused, and years later you still can't breathe. It feels like the structure of your life is crumbling.

Real or imagined, cracks are showing up everywhere. That's the bad news.

Here's the good news: the cracks are a sign, not a conclusion.[4] They are the GPS, not the destination. Whatever pain, fear, anxiety, disruption, or chaos you have in your life—no matter how much it hurts—it's not the final answer. These cracks are shadows of something deeper going on in your life.

Cracks can signal the beginning of the end: A windshield. The mortar between the bricks on a decaying old house. A shattered window in an abandoned building.

Or cracks can signal growth: Old skin making way for new skin. A butterfly leaving a cocoon. A bird breaking free from the egg.

---

4. If you'll allow me, I'm going to beat the "cracks" metaphor to death.

Cracks allow light into the darkness.

Even though I didn't know it, my moment in the mud was the beginning of something new. A new adventure toward strength, health, and healing. In the years following, I became determined to figure out what was wrong with me, my friends, my students, my family, and my country. I became obsessed with getting to the bottom of the lies and nonsense you and I have been told about mental health, wellness, relationships, happiness—and what makes the good life.

In my search to find out why everyone is struggling, I found that almost everything we've been told is wrong.

This Book

This book is about stories. The stories you were born into, the stories you were told, the stories that happened, and the stories you tell yourself. Make no mistake: these stories have a physical weight. We carry them everywhere we go and they impact our bodies, our minds, our communities, and our family tree. They become our mental and physical health, our family systems, our faith, and our future. The stories are both the problem and the solution.

I wrote this book to offer clear and simple insights into our deepest hurts. I also wrote this book to teach you how to live a better life, how to be well, and how to have incredible relationships. As you read, you will learn how to examine and own your old stories, how to heal and write new stories, and how to change the rest of your life. I want you to begin living a strong, whole, well, resilient, and connected life ...

Starting now.

The path to being well and changing your life is simple—just five steps repeated over and over and over again. The five steps are:

1. Own your stories
2. Acknowledge reality
3. Get connected
4. Change your thoughts
5. Change your actions

That's it.

I know, I know . . . don't roll your eyes. Don't move on yet.

Yes, these steps sound simplistic. They *are* simple. But this path is hard to walk. Incredibly hard.

Most people never try. Of those who try, few keep going. If we're speaking statistically, you probably won't go for it. I hope you will, but changing your life is not for the faint of heart.

You have to come clean and be honest. You have to face and discover things you don't want to. You have to both own your past and be decisive about changing your future. You have to do new things and think new things. There will be times the path to healing hurts deeply.

But if you'll start walking? You will change your life. You'll find freedom. Peace. Laughter. Forgiveness. Great sex and connection. Deep sleep without medication. Physical health. Purpose. Joy and so much love. You will change your family tree.

This journey isn't easy, but picking up this book was an act of bravery. An act of strength. I see your strength, even if you don't see it in yourself. So from here on out, I'm assuming you're all in. Working through this book will change you—and I'm right here with you.

You can own your past and change your life.

The cracks are your new beginning.

Here we go.

CHAPTER 2

Acknowledge Your Stories

S everal years ago I was an administrator at a university in Texas. I served on the university's Emergency Response Team (ERT), a small, multi-disciplinary team that dealt with various student crises. One Friday afternoon we were called together after a mini-bus carrying our students was involved in a horrific accident. The wreck involved a university faculty member and a number of students. They'd been headed to an orphanage to spend the weekend serving children.[5]

The single-vehicle accident happened in the middle of nowhere on the backroads of Texas. The wreck scene was a disaster, with students, wallets, backpacks, clothes, and bus parts strewn all over the grassy field by the interstate. Because of the location of the wreck, multiple police departments, state troopers, EMS, and other emergency responders showed up to help.

Anyone who has ever been involved in such a scene knows how confusing and contradictory the flow of information can be.

---

5. Yeah, I know. College students traveling to serve orphans are not supposed to be in fatal car crashes. I still struggle with this.

Everyone has a story—or rather, a piece of it. Media, friends, other students, families, emergency responders, local churches, and school administrators all grasp for bits of information, desperate for details and explanations. Thousands of people exchange stories of what happened, passing along rumors or eyewitness accounts via text messages or social media posts or phone calls or hastily thrown together news broadcasts. Those bits of information get woven into narratives that take on lives of their own, morphing into half-truths and full truths and untruths. The rumors and stories send people running, sometimes solving for problems that don't exist.

It was a long, long night full of tragic stories, inaccurate stories, confirmed stories, retracted stories, and survivor stories. Our students ended up in five different hospitals, hundreds of miles from campus. Some students were taken by ambulance while some were flown by helicopter. And because some students canceled their trip last minute, and others chose to hop on the bus on a whim, we didn't even know who was on the bus and who wasn't.

The night was chaos.

The ERT members met at the university police station and huddled around a large whiteboard. The Chief of Police took command of the room. He divided the board into three vertical columns—alive students, deceased students, and students whose whereabouts were still unknown.[6] We had been informed of at least three

---

6. The fog of multi-victim vehicle accidents is very real. These types of scenes are unimaginably chaotic, especially when there are multiple precincts, multiple individual responders, and multiple EMS units on scene. In the immediate aftermath of a tragedy like this, the priority is getting people to the hospitals for emergency care. The responder's job is to save lives—and worry about information, details, and phone calls later. While early reports from the scene were that three students passed away, when the dust finally cleared, only one remarkable young woman lost her life. It is critically important in these chaotic emergencies to search for facts while holding unconfirmed data loosely.

"known" fatalities, but details were still sketchy. People were scattered all over the state.

I spent the evening and into the night on the phone with parents and siblings who were looking for their loved ones—family members who thought their kids might be *dead*. I talked to parents who drove several hours to one rural county hospital, only to be told their child was somewhere else. After rushing into the emergency room, they had to run back out to the parking lot, jump in their car, and drive to another hospital in another city. Students were in emergency surgery, and other students were already home. Some had severe injuries, some had broken bones—all had broken hearts.

It was a mess.

In the days to come, every student on the bus and their family was assigned a university official. Our job was to walk alongside the student during their recovery and to serve as a liaison between the student's family and the university's resources. We worked hard to make sure they felt cared for and never felt left out of the loop, especially during the haze of the first few weeks of recovery.

I was assigned to an extraordinary family from out of state. When we met for the first time, they were lovely, kind, and understandably shaken. After meeting for an hour or two in a campus office, the student's mother told me she had one final question to ask.

"Go for it," I said.

She sat pensively for a moment and then asked, "The wreck happened in the early afternoon. My child was driven to one hospital and then taken to yet another hospital. Y'all [the university] didn't call us until 11:00 that night. We had no idea that our daughter was hurt until she called us herself, using a nurse's cell phone. Why in the world did you wait so long?"

I inhaled sharply and exhaled through a long pause. I asked her if she wanted a truthful answer or if she just wanted the company line.

Of course she wanted the truth.

I took another long, deep breath.

I told her that early in our emergency debriefing, we were told a number of stories by supposed eyewitnesses—emergency responders and fellow students. One of the first stories we were told, reported by multiple people, was that *her* child was dead.

Her daughter's picture had been taped up in column two: deceased. The delay was simply us waiting for law enforcement officials to get their confirmations in order. Late into the night, when we found out her daughter was alive, we immediately called home.

After I explained what happened, a stunned silence fell over the room.

I will remember the weight of that silence for the rest of my life.

It was the silence of a family's gratitude that their child was still alive. The silence of knowing their daughter had been presumed dead. The silence of our collective grief that someone else's child *had* died.

For the days leading up to our meeting, the family's story was that my team and I were incompetent. Or sloppy. Or scared to make the hard call. It's understandable. The family had experienced stories of fear and horror and unknowing. They'd experienced stories of relief, sadness, and joy. There were stories of what could have been, what was, and what might be.

In some cases, their stories were right. Thankfully, some of their stories were wrong.

In the days and years ahead, everything became about the stories.

The Solution Is in the Stories

What happened with my students on the interstate was a tragedy. A horrendous nightmare.

Kids were badly hurt. A young woman lost her life. Families and emergency responders were changed forever. There were countless speculative stories about what happened and why it happened. There was also a dark and hard reality to what happened. It took months to untangle the mechanics of the wreck, and it will take years to untangle the spiritual, emotional, psychological, and physical impact of the tragedy. There were thousands of personal stories, reflections, and experiences.

And while this wreck was a unique example, I need you to see—and internalize: This is also your life. This is my life too. We've all experienced and continue to experience stories of all shapes and sizes. Our lives are chaotic, unexpected, tragic, boring, joyful, and messy.

We've experienced chaos in our homes, childhood neglect, grief, or loneliness.

We've been cheated on, dumped, hit, or fired.

We are born into systems that deny us equality or connection or opportunity. We are born into homes with both parents or one parent or no parents. Our parents are addicted. Our loved ones suddenly pass away, or they are slowly buried by grief or cancer.

We live off food stamps or food delivery. Our schools are good or awful.

We are the wrong color. From the wrong side of the world. We went to the wrong church or worshiped in the wrong way. We were raped or assaulted or lied to. We were told to shut up or disappear.

Or we were told we are better than other people. That we're the right color. That we can run fast and jump high. We're taught to blame everyone and everything else.

Our lives are a tangled web of stories of what could have been, what was, what is, and what might be.

You have been hurt. I have been hurt. Some of us have been hurt in deeply tragic ways. Others have been hurt in smaller, incremental ways. You've had painful experiences I could never imagine or understand. And this is where we meet—at the intersection of our pain and the rest of our lives.

To move forward, we have to understand that our pain is in the stories.

Stories carry the pain from day to day, from person to person, from generation to generation. The stories become expressed in our genes, trapped in our bodies, and realized in our thoughts and actions.

The solutions to your hurt, to being well, and to changing your life are not about focusing on the villains and the people who hurt you.

The solutions are in the stories.

Stay with me.

No, stories don't pull triggers. They don't steal or swing fists. Stories don't abuse, and they don't scream at or hit children.

But stories do inform how we organize and experience the world. They tell us what it all means.

Our stories become our identity and our filter for how we see, hear, feel, and act. They tell us who is good and what is bad. They can lift us or they can bury us. Some stories come to us as cultural narratives like: a bigger house with more stuff is better. Some stories come to us from people we know and love, like when Dad told us we can do hard things or when Mom told us pudgy little girls and boys aren't lovable. Some stories come to us because they actually happened, like your dad bailing when you were nine or your mom's prescription pill addiction.

And it's the stories that drag the pain of our past into the present, casting scripts that we mindlessly repeat. The stories keep us trapped in toxic patterns, relationships, and ecosystems.

What's tricky about stories is how they move in and out of our lives unnoticed. Stories are like the air we breathe—and most of us have no idea we're inhaling them. Stories are our operating systems—always running in the background.

We have thoughts and believe they're true.

We're told about our worth, and we just accept it.

We're told we're not handsome or smart, and we internalize it.

We're told winning will make us well, and we just keep running faster and harder and more intensely, without any intentionality or understanding about what it will feel like when we get wherever it is we're going.

The stories keep us fighting or sprinting in directions we never intended to go, at speeds we can't keep up. We aim for standards that simply don't exist.

And everyone's got stories. Leaders and millionaires and doctors have stories. So do single moms, teachers, plumbers, and administrative assistants. Exhausted parents, anxious teenagers, burned-out police officers, and sixty-year-old dads too. We all have stories.

So when I talk about stories, I'm talking about you.

And I'm talking about me.

We all have to turn and face the stories. The good ones and the devastating ones.

When we take ownership of our stories, we get to determine what happens next.

Changing the Focus

So much energy is spent blaming, screaming, hating, and seeking to burn everything down—and nothing changes.

The story we've been told is if everyone else will change, life will be better. If only *they* would stop. If *they* would repent. If *they* were destroyed/removed/damaged/silenced, then we would finally be okay. And so we spend our days and years in battle, and the fire burns and the ashes pile up and up and up. And this is where I want to change our cultural and personal obsession with trying to fill internal holes with external plugs. Finding someone new to hate has never solved anything. It just ends in piles of bodies.

I spent years blaming everyone and everything and trying to solve every external problem like a rage-fueled game of Whack-a-mole. I spent every last ounce of energy trying to fix and fight every crisis and every system, and I spent all my intellectual and leadership capital trying to create a policy to address every discomfort and bruised feeling. All my energy went toward looking for cracks around me, without ever bothering to look in the mirror.

I was the common denominator of my pain. I was at war with myself.

I never once acknowledged the stories I was born into, the stories I was told, the stories that happened, or the stories I was telling myself. I wasn't honest about my own role in my life. I just chased every bad or frustrating or annoying or achievement-oriented gold star I could get my hands on. Nothing got better. The problem was the stories.

In his classic masterpiece *Man's Search for Meaning*, Viktor Frankl says, "When we are no longer able to change a situation, we are challenged to change ourselves."[7] And changing ourselves means looking in the mirror and dealing with the stories.

So from this point forward, we will turn and face the stories. We will own them. You will own yours, and I will own mine. This is the first step on the path to healing and wholeness.

Types of Stories

As I've mentioned, there are four types of stories that direct our lives:

- **The stories we're born into**—cultural narratives, political histories, churches and faith heritage, and family identities and traditions. This is the air we breathe.
- **The stories others tell us**—our worth, value, and ability. Told to us by our institutions, our parents and teachers, our enemies, and friends.
- **The stories that actually happen**—we got fired, she said yes, someone in our unit died, someone else got the job, the baby got sick, we had twins, or the economy collapsed. These stories are about reality.
- **The stories we tell ourselves**—the ones about identity and who we are. The judgments we cast on ourselves.

Whether we realize it or not, these stories shape how we walk into a room and what we say when we get there. They inform the clothes we wear and the cars we drive, where we live and work, and how we spend our free time. They masquerade as our assumptions and biases. They direct where we focus our attention, and they tell

---

7. Viktor E. Frankl, *Man's Search for Meaning*, (Boston: Beacon Press, 2006), 112.

our bodies when to run, fight, or feel safe. They direct other people on how they can maintain power or control.

Stories can be good and beautiful and right. Some are uncomfortable, yet true. Some stories are based in unchangeable, cast-in-stone reality.

A few stories stand the test of time.

And now, thanks to all our technology and progress, we're bombarded with countless stories piped directly into our minds. Stories used to be powered by your family of origin, local religion, and maybe a man yelling in the town square. Now they're powered by social media, algorithms, and Tesla.

Owning the Stories

During those years when my head was on fire, I was slowly killing myself and didn't know it.

I was just following the stories I'd been handed. These stories told me more and faster was better, and entitlement was truth.

The stories told me my discomfort was always someone else's fault and everyone else needed to change in order for my life to get better. The stories told me my childhood traumas were my fault.

They told me the world owed me a perfect job that wasn't too hard. That pain can be avoided if we can just make the right rules and the right policies.

The stories said I could yell and fight my way to wellness. To peace. To happiness.

The stories told me my self-worth was based on accomplishment. That my value was found in expertise and how much money I made. That God owed me healthy children and a perfect marriage and low interest rates on my mortgage.

The stories said I could do it all without having to make hard choices. The stories said do more, get more, sleep less, and crush all obstacles.

Stories also told me that if I ever stumbled, got hurt, or got scared, I could just numb, scroll, eat, lift, hunt and fish, video game, smoke, golf, drink, Netflix, flirt, gossip, or study myself away from reality.

The story said: Just. Keep. Going.

So I kept going. Faster and faster.

But I never asked myself the magic question . . .

What do I want for my one, short, precious life?

What was I running from? What was I running toward? Where was I going?

Toward crazier fun? More meetings? Nicer suits? A recliner? Retirement? More shoes? A bigger deer hunt? Better abs? More money? Kids that did whatever I said? The opportunity to finally do whatever I wanted to do, with whatever tread was left on the tires?

Imagine my shock when I realized I was running hard but going nowhere. That my anger and rage were never about solving problems—they were just about anger and rage. And that I was teaching my young son to keep this thing going—so he could pass it on to his kids.

I was just following the stories I was told. And I was paying dearly for it.

That night in the West Texas mud and rain, I began to acknowledge that I was living a story that wasn't true. Getting well was still many months (and even years) away, but the first step to getting well was recognizing I'd been following the wrong stories. Lots of them.

My house was never cracking apart. It was just a story I was telling myself. And even if there were cracks, it didn't mean financial ruin. Finding cracks in a new home didn't mean I was a bad husband or a failed father. These were stories about shame and catastrophe. This was a story about isolation and ego. And on and on.

Pioneering psychologist Rollo May said that "courage, whether the soldier's courage in risking death or the child's in going off to school, means the power to let go of the familiar and the secure. Courage is required not only in a person's occasional crucial decision for his own freedom, but in the little hour-to-hour decisions."[8]

It was time for me to be courageous.

To the shock of those around me and even to myself, I stepped back from the stories—from the ladder climbing and the grind. If you've ever been an actor on a stage, you know the thrill and fear of being off-book. Of being out there with no notes—just you and the audience.

I was officially off-book. No script. No more guiding stories.

I began examining my old stories one by one. I tossed the old ones in the fire pit. With the help of my wife, friends, professionals, mentors, and countless personal challenges, I started imagining and writing new stories. I went back to the old roads and started from there. I found freedom and joy and wellness in owning my old stories . . . and in writing new ones.

Your Next Step

As we walk together through these pages, remember: focus on the stories.

When I look at our world—at the hatred and dysfunction and disastrous mental, physical, and spiritual health—my heart breaks. All we did was believe the stories. We followed the recommendations

---

8. Rollo May, *Man's Search for Himself,* (New York: W.W. Norton & Company, 1953), 173.

of our government, of the media, of the scientists and the other experts who we thought cared about us. And actually, many of them did care about us. They still do. They were just living and passing *their* stories along, whether they meant to or not.

My heart breaks for what happened to you when you were six, and I'm heartbroken that you feel trapped in an abusive marriage. I am heartbroken for the stories that told you I was your enemy, that you don't look the right way, and that violence and shame are normal.

I'm heartbroken over all of it.

But here we are.

Right now.

Today.

And this book is about your very next step. It's about what happens next.

We have to look at the stories.

We're going to start examining the stories you're living—the ones you were born into, the ones you've been told, the ones that actually happened, and the ones you tell yourself. We're going to take both the red pill and the blue pill at the same time and begin to see the world for what it truly is.

And as I said before, this is going to hurt. Depending on your personal experiences, the next few chapters might be brutal. As you become aware of your stories, you can feel discouraged. Angry. Heartbroken. When you start pulling on one thread, the entire sweater can quickly unravel. You might even want to stick your head back in the sand and return to the stories that feel comfortable. Sometimes known pain feels safer than an unknown tomorrow. That's normal.

I've been there too.

But stay with me.

If you hang in there, you *will* find the light. And the light will find you. And that's when everything changes. Others have walked these old roads before you, and you will find good company along the way. You'll find that the light has been shining on you the whole time.

Three Lines in the Sand

Before we move on, I want to draw three important lines in the sand. I welcome and expect dissent and raised eyebrows. I love finding out where I've been wrong.

But I want to make sure you and I are clear before moving on.

First, the point of this book is not deconstruction. My goal is not that you end up with a pile of yarn and no sweater. This book is about how you can change your life, be well and whole, and have extraordinary relationships. We have some excavating to do, but the goal is to design and rebuild something new and stronger than ever.

Second, it is important to note that each of the sections in the next few chapters are *entire fields of study*. Where I might address a story you've been born into in a page or two, a motivated person could earn a PhD and spend their entire lives studying the individual subject. My purpose in the next few chapters is high-level awareness—not deep dives, complexity, or nuanced dissertations. I often find that people who are avoiding hard truths come up with complex academic gymnastics or nitpicking to avoid looking in the mirror. I know because I do it all the time. So let me be clear: I'm not an expert in any of these individual spaces. I have had to lean on other experts, personal experiences, and research journals—as well as write in a way that doesn't cause you to pass out from boredom. As you're reading, remember to think big picture, and don't spin your tires.

And finally, I have spent more than twenty years working in educational and mental health settings advocating for and supporting people on the margins. I have worked closely with individuals, groups, families, and scholars. And while I can never internalize their experiences, I have had the honor of listening to real traumas and walking alongside folks with real challenges. This book is not a dismissal of real trauma, both historical and current. It's about freedom. I am not avoiding the truth; I am daring to walk right into the heart of it. I am not letting systems or evil people off the hook; I am just turning the lights on for everyone, everywhere.

Additionally, keep in mind that it isn't possible to list out every single story every person faces. What you'll find in these pages is a sampling of examples to illustrate how stories operate in our lives. If I don't mention your particular situation, know that I'm neither dismissing your pain or letting you off the hook. I'm for you, not against you.

Remember: both the problems and the solutions are in the stories.

If you're interested in going deeper in any or all of these areas, I have noted some of the world's foremost thought leaders and important books on the related topics in the back of this book. If a particular story (or three or four) rings true to you, I highly recommend you check out those experts and learn from people who have spent their lives researching and writing in these specialized areas. If a particular story or issue sounds like nonsense to you and makes you roll your eyes, just move on to the next topic.

And finally, some of you are not ready for this book. That's okay. I realize I'm dumping everything you know on its head and I'm going to expect a lot of you. There are no hacks, magic pills, quick fixes, or big groups to blame that will heal you or make everything instantly better.

If you're not ready yet, I still love you and I'm glad you walked with us this far. Feel free to just set the book down and come back to it later—or give it to someone else.[9]

But if you're ready to change everything, to be free and begin a new adventure in healing, turn the page. Your time is here.

_____

9. Or if there are still energy or toilet paper shortages where you live, it might serve as decent kindling and less-than-decent two-ply if you find yourself in a pinch.

CHAPTER 3

Stories About the World

Anna Del Priore was born in 1912—the same year the *Titanic* sank.[10] She caught the Spanish Flu when she was six and Covid-19 when she was one hundred and seven.

Let that sink in[11] for a minute.

Think about what Anna has seen in her lifetime.

World War I, World War II, Vietnam, Korea, Desert Storm, and the Afghanistan and Iraq wars.

She watched the evolution from handwritten letters to telegrams to switchboard operators to phone booths to rotary phones to cordless phones to satellite phones to mobile phones to smart watches. From small family vegetable gardens to having anything she wants delivered to her front door, including wild salmon caught thousands of miles away.

---

10. Two important things about *Titanic*: 1) Jack could have fit on that door, but Rose kept him off. Plot twist: Rose was a murderer. 2) She *did* let go. She let Jack freeze to death, and then she just dropped him, all the way to the bottom of the ocean.

11. No pun intended.

Anna was born into a very different story than we live in now. In a little more than a century, her world experienced an explosion of connection, innovation, and gadgets. She has seen the world get faster, more responsive, safer, and more interconnected. She has also seen the world get slower, sicker, far more dangerous, and lonelier.

And her world is our world.

Over the past three hundred years, the world has shifted underneath us in extraordinary ways. We've *ooo'd* and *ahhh'd* at the shiny new things, but most of us haven't stopped to take it all in. Make no mistake: the transformations have been astonishing. I'm grateful for instant global connectivity, advances in prenatal care, and air conditioning. I'm grateful that we have solved for a vast amount of human suffering, gluten-free gummy bears, and digital streaming.

But if we're honest, we will admit that the extraordinary is only half of the story.

We were born into stories about how our bodies, hearts, minds, and souls work. We've been told nature is too slow, our ancestors were too dumb, and God is for the unenlightened. We've been told to live for today and if it can't be quantified and measured, it's not real.

The stories told us to believe that our smarts and technology would make everything better. That just the right program or algorithm would solve sadness, loneliness, and mental health issues. But then I look at the global mental health crisis, disastrous physical and psychological health in advanced countries, global debt, decreasing lifespans in the United States, and the existential crises surrounding some of most important societal pillars: education, faith, and government.

Things are not as they should be.

Over the past few centuries, we've traded speed for rigor; innovation for wisdom; achievement for sanity; technology for connection; and disconnection for immediate comfort. And we're all paying the price.

The Stories of Our Ecosystem

In this chapter, we're going to focus on a few of the stories we've been born into—the ones that quietly dictate much of our existence and that we largely take for granted. Just as the gardener working with distressed plants starts by examining the quality of the sun exposure, water, and soil, we must start this journey by looking at our ecosystem.

Our ecosystem includes our home, business, body, culture, community, family, and friends. Our ecosystem is also made up of stories that tell us what is normal, what is good or bad, and how we should live.

If we're going to look at the world we live in, we have to be honest about the whole story—especially about what *isn't* working. There's a lot about our incredible world that isn't so incredible anymore.

Here are some uncomfortable truths: We have virtually unlimited connectivity and access to everything and everyone. We also have unlimited access to entertainment on demand, food on demand, and a global supply of stuff, ready to be delivered to our door. Never before in the history of the world have we been more interconnected at both the local and global level.

Yet strangely, this unlimited easy access to everyone and everything has not made us happier or more well. Instead, we've become dangerously lonely and angry, feeling constantly victimized and under attack. We no longer spend time together or discuss ideas—we click and post and lob soundbites at one another. We listen to idiotic influencers and ignore experts. Some experts sell out for financial gain. We overeat, over-consume, over-avoid, and otherwise chase our tails.

But forget connecting with other people and other things. We don't even connect with ourselves anymore. Most people I talk to don't like who they see in the mirror. We're too fat. Too thin. Too bald. Too hairy. Not good enough. Too much trauma. Not enough love. We don't make enough money or didn't go to the right schools.

But we *have* everything. So much stuff. So many degrees. Countless opportunities. So much access to so much information. And yet the residents of the world's wealthiest nations are inexplicably dying younger. We're suffocating under diseases of despair, including an unprecedented spike in addiction, suicide, cancers, and heart disease.[12]

Why are we dying younger, more miserable, more in debt, and more mentally, physically, spiritually, and relationally unwell?

While the stories around us have changed . . . *we have not.*

Our brains, bodies, and spirits are running on ancient technology,[13] dropped into a ludicrous-speed world, trying to stumble through our lives on a cocktail of day drinking, swipe-rights, antidepressants, Benzos, sleeping pills, pornography, kids' activities, and additional square footage. Maybe just the right countertops or job title or lover will take the edge off the burn. I just need a new job, a new town, or a new president to make it all better. We're going too fast and in too many directions.

---

12. Paul Conti, M.D., "Episode #15–Paul Conti, M.D.: trauma, suicide, community, and self-compassion," *The Drive* podcast by Peter Attia, September 17, 2018, https://peterattiamd.com/paulconti/.

13. I despise technology and industrial metaphors to describe human beings. We're not machines and we're not computers, and when we think of ourselves as a piece of metal or a piece of tech, we make unrealistic conclusions about who we are and what we're capable of. But I must admit, it does make for easily understood metaphors, so alas, I caved in this time and just went with it.

We're trying to jam an electric car charger into the backside of the mule pulling our buggy.

It's not working.

The Stories Changed

What's important in this discussion is not the innovations or the actual changes themselves. What matters is how *the stories* of the past three hundred or so years have changed. The stories that inform and dictate the way we live, telling us what's "important" or "truthful" or "necessary" or "normal" or "the right way to do things." As Dr. Ian Malcom mused in the original *Jurassic Park* film, "Scientists were so preoccupied with whether or not they could, they didn't stop to think if they should." But this isn't just about scientists. It's about culture and faith and entertainment and technology. We could, so we did.

And here we are.

Now, I'm not a nostalgic guy. As I said before, I'm grateful for this time in history. I like eating avocadoes in February and not having to build a fire every time I want dinner. I'm not the guy standing on the street corner selling doomsday papers and building bomb shelters. Please don't mistake what I'm saying here.

Our problem isn't progress or even the pace of progress. Our problem is one of *story*. Of *identity*.

In centuries past, our lives were built around our small communities—finding enough to eat, mating and building families, all while trying to stay warm and not get eaten or conquered. Comfort was relative and rare. Meaning and purpose were centered around staying alive, helping others stay alive, and making sure the gods didn't flood or burn the place down. There was only one story: survival. Survival included lunch, procreation, and worship.

This was our story for centuries. For better or worse, it told us who we were. What clothes to wear. Who did what jobs. Who was important and who wasn't. This story helped cultures and societies survive, thrive, or perish.

Today in most parts of the world, we appear to have solved for survival. Of course, calamities can turn this security on its head in an instant, but for billions of people across the globe, our stories are now about purpose, meaning, and efficiency. We are told stories of freedom and "find your passion" and "follow your dreams" and "you can do anything you want." Our new stories are about minimum effective doses and never feeling uncomfortable.

These stories are a blessing and a privilege, and I'm grateful that I get to live in this little sliver of history. But we have to understand that no matter how amazing these new stories are, they come with consequences.

For the rest of this chapter and the next two, we're going to examine some of the major storylines of our ecosystem—the ones we were born into—that are tragically out of balance with our physical, mental, and spiritual bodies. I could have picked any number of stories, but I zeroed in on three recurring versions that I see over and over. Stories about what will save us, stories about ourselves, and stories about others. Remember, the goal is not to get hung up on the nuances of the stories, but to step back and take in the big picture. I want you to begin to see—to feel in your bones—that the stories we've accepted as normal might not be so normal after all.

Story 1: Technology and Innovation Will Save Us

We've been born into a story that technology can fix everything. From aging to food to friendship to disease—technology can, will, and must save us. The story is that the faster and easier and more connected things are, the happier, healthier, and more connected we will be! Life will be easier. Simpler. *Better.*

In some ways this is true. Innovations in housing, energy, agriculture, transportation, medical care, and other fields have led to an explosion of real gains that benefit billions of people every day. For the moment, the world is safer, with less hunger and more money. But we're dancing on a razor's edge.

Digital technology now undergirds everything we do. The algorithms. The networks. The grids. The supply chains and missing computer chips. The constant push for smaller, faster, and better innovation. Just a few companies decide which voices are heard and which ones are not. Our TVs listen to us, our dishwashers turn themselves on, our phones tell us when to wake up and when to go to sleep. Digital calendars, transportation, food production, and reporting tools dictate our lives. Companies are buying and selling information about where I look online, what I read, where I go, and what I buy. My eyes, ears, and brain are now part of a multibillion-dollar Attention Economy.[14]

Technology allows me to sell my organs while I'm still alive.

My devices allow me to be connected and work all the time. I'm never out of reach from my wife, my kids, my friends, and my work. My relationships are no longer context specific—they are everywhere. Work is no longer confined to work—I can do it anywhere, always. You can too. So we take our work and relationships with us everywhere. Home. And to the gym. And in our cars. And on vacation. And hiking in the woods. We've ended up working *more*, not

---

14. BER staff, "Paying Attention: The Attention Economy," *Berkeley Economic Review*, March 31, 2020, https://econreview.berkeley.edu/paying-attention-the-attention-economy/.

less. It's considered rude not to respond to every text, email, and phone message from a friend or loved one.

Work and relationships are now harder, not easier.

During the great Covid shutdown of 2020, we all worked from home. We all worked way more, and we all got way less done. We never unplugged. We never stopped working. We got to work from home, but we never got to go home from work.

So now we live less and try to accomplish and respond more. All of a sudden the technology that was supposed to free our schedules ended up taking our souls. We became skilled multi-taskers until researchers proved that multitasking wasn't real.[15] But we plowed ahead.

Social media promised it would help build connection. It would connect ideas, extend humanitarian care, and serve as a digital thread of love woven into the fabric of society. We were one big happy family waiting to all be plugged in together.

But instead of coming together digitally to work and solve for local and regional challenges, we're overwhelmed by the relentless waves of negative news related to inequality, systemic failures, racism, vast wealth disparities, generational traumas, and reports of people trying to destroy democracy. And while I'm at it, I can spend all day comparing my body, my smarts, my accomplishments, my perceived economic situation, and my overall value with millions of curated people—all at the same time.

Our bodies are never safe trying to empathize, solve, fight, or flee from the never-ending onslaught of personal and global despair.

The problem is, technology doesn't solve our deepest spiritual or existential problems—it magnifies what's already there. It

---

15. Anthony D. Wagner and Melina R. Uncapher, "Minds and brains of media multitaskers: Current findings and future directions," *PNAS*, October 2, 2018, https://www.pnas.org/content/115/40/9889.full.

accelerates and amplifies them. It allows us to attend a funeral virtually, grieving with loves ones while being totally alone.

This is disconnection.

And again, technology isn't bad. It's not moral and it doesn't have character. It's just a bunch of ones and zeros. But you and I have to understand that our brains, bodies, spirits, and emotions aren't designed to be in this many places at once. We have to internalize how worshiping technology and innovation has sped us up, changed how we communicate, how we work, how we consume information, and how we create and share knowledge.

This story changed everything all at once.

And there is a dark side. Oh yeah, it gets worse.

My life savings can now be drained by a teenager with a laptop on some island in the Pacific. Companies record voice calls and text messages without your knowledge[16] and create voice-identifying, click-inducing, and brain-hacking echo chambers. Technology allows data companies to create psychometric maps of our kids' brains through standardized testing and to extract the last drops of free will out of our very human lives.[17] While some are using technology to solve problems, others are using it to create incomprehensibly dystopian realities.

We're living in a sci-fi movie, but our ancient brains are still trying to find a mate and not get eaten.

And the innovations aren't slowing down. We're on the cusp of a technological acceleration unlike anything this world has ever seen: Gene editing. Millions of fertilized fetuses in storage. The end

---

16. Or unceremoniously and intentionally buried in some tiny-font'd Terms of Use somewhere.

17. Maybe a bit over the top, maybe not. But there's a lot of research on standardized testing with our kids and how that information and data is being used. Fascinating but also scary at the same time.

of the Great Stagnation.[18] The internet of things. Artificial intelligence and machine learning. Predator vs. Alien. Terminator 2, 3, and 4—or something like that.

And the experts say we haven't even started yet.

The story we were born into is that technology and innovation can solve all our problems, even our most challenging personal, nutritional, spiritual, and existential ones.

This story has turned out to be tragically untrue.

Story 2: Debt Will Save Us

There is more money circulating the world economies than ever before in human history. And by money I don't mean coins or currency specifically. I'm talking more about wealth, resources, purchasing power—the ability to get whatever we want, whenever we want it.

In our current economic systems, we pretend there's no limit to the amount of money or wealth that we can whip up, print, and direct deposit. We've created countless digital currencies. Some smart folks just made it up with their laptops while listening to chillhop and riding hoverboards.[19] During the Covid pandemic, the US government printed trillions of dollars on both sides of the election. They just waved a magic wand like Harry Potter. Or Oprah.

You get a check! And you get a check! And you get a check!

---

18. Tyler Cowen, "Me on the end of the Great Stagnation," *Marginal Revolution*, April 26, 2021, https://marginalrevolution.com/?s=great+stagnation.

19. I really have no idea who was brilliant enough to come up with Bitcoin and blockchains and other digital currencies, or how they did it. I just imagine they were way, way cooler than me. And I'm just guessing here, but they probably have hoverboards and mustaches.

But it's even bigger than that.

Think Google. A few decades ago, there was no Google. It didn't exist. We had to use a dictionary or an encyclopedia.[20] Then a couple guys started tinkering with algorithms in their garage, and *boom*—a few years later they had a trillion-dollar organization. Actually, the *world* had a trillion-dollar organization. That wealth was added to the global economy almost like pixie dust.

The same story goes for Apple, Amazon, Uber, and countless others. Enron went away. So did Blockbuster. But Netflix, Microsoft, and Tesla sprouted and grew. So did pharmaceutical companies, healthcare conglomerates, and massive insurance companies. And things are continuing to morph at unfathomable speeds.

As of this writing, Airbnb is the largest hospitality company in the world, yet they own no real estate. Not a single home. Uber is the largest transportation company in the world, yet they do not own a single vehicle. DoorDash is a massive food delivery company that does not cook a single meal. Craigslist doesn't sell anything. Angie doesn't fix anything.

Things are changing.

We've created so much wealth, value, goods, services, educated people, business, conveniences, and endless shell games for paying for it. The brilliant Tyler Cowan suggests there are more educated, creative people who have access to endless resources than ever before in the history of the world.

That's good news. Right?

Yes, and . . .

Very few people have the freedom to invest the money they earn.

---

20. Or just let that one idiot at the party keep making up sports stats or dinosaur facts or apocalypse predictions. (You weren't that dude, right?)

Everything is leveraged and leaning on everything else. Countries owe themselves and other countries. There is no anchored currency except to someone else's currency. On a global scale, we have borrowed and restructured and created tools for consuming without paying the piper.

When we look back at the early twentieth century, personal debt was a curse. Even into the 1950s,[21] American families earned as much as they could in a given year and they generally spent a little less than they earned. The idea of spending *more* than you earned—not to mention significantly more than you earned—was considered irresponsible and insane. Everyone knew debt was slavery. Debt was considered a last resort of tragic proportions.

But after World War II, once people came home and got to work, the story of debt-as-slavery began to change. Currency became a commodity. Debt became seen as a tool or an opportunity.

Why wait until tomorrow when you could have it today?! Invariably, store credit and credit cards were born. And what was once considered a move of desperation is now considered normal and the smart choice. Barely seventy years later we find the average US family holding at least three credit cards.[22] Households with at least one card carry an average of $14,821 of credit card debt.[23] Altogether, the total consumer debt for US households is a whopping 15 trillion

21. Daniel Indiviglio, "How Americans' Love Affair with Debt Has Grown," *The Atlantic,* September 26, 2010, https://www.theatlantic.com/business/archive/2010/09/how-americans-love-affair-with-debt-has-grown/63552/.

22. Stefani Wendel, "State of Credit 2020: Consumer Credit During COVID-19," *Experian,* October 20, 2020, https://www.experian.com/blogs/insights/2020/10/state-credit-2020/.

23. Federal Reserve Bulletin, "Changes in U.S. Family Finances from 2016-2019: Evidence from the Survey of Consumer Finances," *Federal Reserve,* September 2020, https://www.federalreserve.gov/publications/files/scf20.pdf and United States Census Bureau, https://data.census.gov/cedsci/.

dollars—mostly from mortgages, student loans, auto loans, and credit cards.[24]

That is a staggering number when you think about it. Fifteen trillion dollars of imaginary money. IOUs.

Trust me, I'm good for it.

I'll pay you back . . . I swear.

The blood pumping through the heart and veins of the world's economy is not real. Everybody owes everybody.

Experts on both sides of the aisle provide numerous perspectives on why people are so addicted to debt. We want new cars. Housing is too expensive. No one lives on a budget and there is no self-discipline. Everybody is supposed to go to college, and colleges are doubling their tuition every seven to ten years. People of means can't say no to more building and more leverage, while others are stuck in cycles of poverty.

For this book, though, I'm less concerned with drilling into the *Why*. I'll leave that to the economists and sociologists. I'm more concerned with turning on the lights, turning off the party music, and taking a stark and honest look at *What is*.

The interconnected web of global debt is fragile and catastrophic. All these pressures and forces that distill down to you and me are relatively new. But what isn't new is that debt has been a known strategy for trapping entire segments of a population. Everyone knew it. Since the beginning of time.

Now, though, we all wake up, hop out of bed, and willfully shackle ourselves to a few banks, a cell phone company, the mall, car dealerships, mortgage companies, and various retail stores. We

---

24. Federal Reserve Bank of New York, "Household Debt and Credit Report (Q3 2021)," *New York Fed,* December 10, 2021, https://www.newyorkfed.org/micro economics/hhdc.html.

even buy T-shirts, jeans with holes in them, and concert tickets on payment plans. We feel entitled to live in certain cities, at certain standards, and with certain lifestyles. Or conversely, we were preyed upon and told a story about what we could accomplish, what life was supposed to look like, or that there was no other way.

Either way, things are a mess.

Working today to pay for something you ate yesterday is *normal*. Making payments on depreciating assets is *normal*. Constructing a financial universe where all of your payments add up to your salary is *normal*. If you don't participate, you're considered an outsider. A troublemaker. A risk.

But owing people is crippling. Anxiety and depression are about a lack of control and autonomy over your future. And few things inhibit control and autonomy over a future like owing people money.

And we owe trillions.

After taking countless calls from listeners and talking to thousands of college students over the years, I've come to believe that a person cannot be psychologically whole or well while owing someone else money.

Owing someone money is like handing them the pen to the story of your life and letting someone else write it for you. They get to write the terms, the deadlines, and the consequences. They get to tell you what you'll eat, where you'll live, and how much time you can spend with loved ones.

The story we've been told is that we got smarter than money. That debt is normal. The story is that currency doesn't have to be tethered to reality. That math works everywhere but in finance. The story is that debt is a tool, not a trap. An opportunity, not a jail cell. The story is, if we run out of money, we'll just print more. Or borrow more. And almost all of us have played along in this fantasy, willingly chaining ourselves to more and more financial obligation and less and less freedom.

The story is that debt will save us. But our brains and bodies are sounding the alarms.

Story 3: I Can Save Myself

One of the most pervasive and insidious stories of the past three hundred years is that you can save yourself, by yourself, and you don't need anyone. What began as a righteous and ordained call for freedom, liberty, and personal responsibility has morphed into a lie. The lie is that you are all that matters. That you can have it all and do it all, all by yourself. That you don't need other people.

The distortion of the ideals of freedom and responsibility, combined with the illusions of technology and debt, has given birth to the most destructive and evil force the world has ever known.

Loneliness.

I grew up on a small suburban street in north Houston, Texas. Our block was blessed with a seemingly endless stream of young kids, all about the same age.

We played made-up sports games together, got in barn-burner fights, broke things (and broke *into* things), stole things, hid things, built things, spent the night at each other's houses, and caused mayhem. We started clubs, mowed lawns, laughed our guts out, wept together, watched movies, ate meals together, camped together, caught snakes and turtles and fish, and nailed each other with pine cones.

These guys were my first friends. My gang.

Over time, our parents moved away. We moved away. We got married and had kids. We became Scout dads or Little League dads or "watch TV" dads.

We all grew apart. We got busy. We stopped hanging out so much and started calling. We stopped calling and started texting. We stopped returning texts immediately. We sent emails.

This also happened with my high school friends and my college friends. They were there . . . and then I blinked. And suddenly an internet algorithm based in San Francisco was sending me reminders that it was someone's birthday. Or their anniversary. A picture would flash on my phone, showing me that someone had a baby. He got divorced. She got promoted. They got laid off.

Right under my nose, the friends I *have* quietly became the friends I *had.*

When I was a kid, I didn't know how to have friends. There were always just other kids around—down the street or on my team or in my class. Friendship wasn't planned or intentional. We just did it. In high school and college too. Same dorms, classes, teams, or interests. People were just around.[25]

But after college I entered the work world and friends stopped "just happening." I had to work for it. And I didn't have the skills or make the time. So my old friends and I tried to prop things up for a while—texting and sending memes and getting together for a drink when one of us was in the other person's town. But within a few years I was doing my things, they were doing their things, and almost overnight I found myself just watching another episode of *The Office.*

Alone.

By the way, the same thing happened with my brother and sister. And my parents. And my in-laws. And my extended family. We

---

25. I also know this is my story and not the case for millions of young people, especially those on the margins who are left out, isolated, or bullied. My point here is that making friends when we're younger is often a matter of environment. We're dropped into classes or neighborhoods or sports teams with other kids. This diminishes as we age.

all got busy. We saw each other on holidays, we shared some laughs, and we moved on.

I didn't know them and they really didn't know me.

It also happened in my marriage. My wife was doing her things and I was doing my things and we were excellent co-managers of the house. I had my dreams and she had hers. She had her lists and I had my diets and plans and exercises and half-baked home improvement projects. We both had grad school.

We loved each other a lot. But without even meaning to, we ended up sitting next to each other on the couch. She was on her digital device and I was on mine.

We were two inches apart and two thousand miles away from each other.

I don't want to be overdramatic here. I had friends at the MMA gym. I had good buddies at work. I hung out with people here and there. I had folks I cared about in my workplaces, and I loved chitchatting with my grad school friends. As I said, I loved my wife and, on most days, she liked me back.[26]

But loneliness was something different. It was a cloud. A weight. It just hung around.

I remembered being lonely as a kid, feeling out of place and being awkward. I lied and exaggerated a lot, had acne, was gangly and goofy, and was generally uncomfortable in my own skin. I had lots of people around, but I always felt one step removed.

And all the stories said I was responsible for me. My personal growth. My development. My attitude. My money. My accomplishments. My schooling and my grades. And so I plowed ahead—grinding, accomplishing, and solving—while my body was sounding the loneliness alarms.

---

26. Let's be honest: I can be a lot.

This sense of loneliness grew as I got older. I was surrounded, yet alone.

All of a sudden, no matter how many friends I had in my phone or on social media, I felt alone. All these years later, I've perfected the art of hiding in a crowded room. Of being alone in bed with my wife. I've mastered the art of just grabbing a drink and being quiet. Of texting funny memes and not authentically reaching out.

I am good at being lonely.

And if I look at the data, I'm confident of a powerful truth:

You're lonely too.

The Loneliness Epidemic

About ten years ago, I became obsessed with the topic of loneliness. How in the world, when I knew so many people and had so many phone numbers, was I still so lonely? I also knew that everyone around me—students and parents and co-workers and neighbors—were lonely too. I read everything I could get my hands on. I met behind closed doors with professionals, clients, and those who society said had "made it." I talked with elite military, professional athletes, professors, speakers, students, and single moms working multiple gigs to pay rent. I traveled the country speaking at academic conferences and connecting with hundreds of students, their families, and their friends.

Over time a picture emerged that I simply couldn't believe: everyone was lonely.

Poor people. Rich people. Extroverted people. Introverted people. Religious people. Atheists. Married people. Single people. Divorced people. People having affairs. People with deep meaning in their work and people who were radically disengaged at work. All of the Enneagram numbers, all of the Myers-Briggs letters, and all of the StrengthsFinder labels. Everyone I talked with was struggling.

We have a thousand friends on the internet and no one to help us move our couch. We have 342 potential customers in our funnel, but no one to help us change a flat tire in our driveway. Or to help move the fridge. Or to keep my kids in the middle of the night when my wife needs to go to the hospital. Couples who have been married for fifteen years have become roommates.

Everybody I talked to was telling me a different version of the same story: they were so, so lonely.

The story said we could save ourselves. But we're not waving, we're drowning.

We are the hotline generation.

Non-profits and government agencies have created artificial connections with strangers when we need help with scary thoughts or dark days because we have no one in our lives we can connect with, be vulnerable with, or turn to.

When was the last time you were surrounded by friends and you laughed so hard your drink came out of your nose?

When's the last time you had an entire conversation made up entirely of movie quotes, song lyrics, or inside jokes?

When was the last time something hurt your feelings or broke your heart and someone showed up just to sit and be silent with you?

That's what I thought.

Awake and Alone

Let's do a little thought experiment. Imagine yourself a thousand years ago, and you and your small tribe are living a nomadic life on the plains of North America. As the sun tucks itself over the horizon, the darkness signals that it's time for everyone to bed down. You close your eyes amidst your community and drift off into a deep sleep.

You jolt awake the following morning to find your tribe missing. Gone. They have all left without you.

No footsteps, no familiar voices, no clanging of tools or sounds of people laughing and eating. Silence.

Just silence.

Instantly your body surges with stress hormones and fight-or-flight chemicals, including cortisol and adrenaline. Your senses become highly attuned. Your pupils dilate as you feverishly scan the horizon. You start running in a general direction. You stop and listen deeply. You run another direction.

Your heart is racing and your skin is tingling with perspiration. Your hearing is attenuated. All these physical sensations are your body sounding the alarm that you're in danger. You're cut off from your lifeblood. From safety. From those who know you. Your body recognizes this danger even before your sluggish brain catches up and registers its terror.

Soon you start to perceive threats and danger everywhere. Little sounds. Snapping twigs. Rustling leaves. Each sound or glimpse sets off aggressive or cowering responses. They prime you to go to war or to retreat and run.

Whether or not you understand it mentally, your body knows that all alone, out here in the grasslands, you are going to die.

Close your eyes for a minute and picture that scene. Be there as best you can. Live that moment for as long as you can stand it.

Now open your eyes.

As we discussed in chapter 2, that brain and body from a thousand years ago is basically the same brain and body you have now. A brain and body that is literally wired for connection. A brain and body that instinctively knows: without other people in your life to love you, protect you, mate with you, and work and worship with you, you won't survive.

And yes, I see you, hard-charging CEO. I see you, multimillionaire lawyer, or doctor, or fancy preacher. I also see you, life-of-the-party who outdrinks, outlaughs, and outperforms everyone else. And I see you, quiet introvert who just wants to go home and have a glass of wine and watch a show . . . exhausted father who is hiding behind the latest football game . . . beautiful soul whose husband just walked out.

I'm talking to you.

You need friends.

Community.

A gang.

Connection.

Places where you can be vulnerable.

Times when you can stop posturing and stop being the strongest/smartest/loudest/quietest person in the room.

We are the loneliest generation in the history of humankind, and that loneliness is killing us.

I know. I get it. Loneliness sounds cliché and cheesy.

But we can't ignore the data.

Loneliness scholars and researchers Drs. Louise Hawkley and John Cacioppo found that "loneliness has been associated with personality disorders and psychoses, suicide, impaired cognitive performance and cognitive decline over time, increased risk of Alzheimer's . . . , and increases in depressive symptoms."[27] Addition-

---

27. Louise C. Hawkley, John T. Cacioppo, "Loneliness Matters: A Theoretical and Empirical Review of Consequences and Mechanisms." *Oxford Academic*, July 22, 2010, https://academic.oup.com/abm/article/40/2/218/4569527.

ally, they found that when the body recognizes it is lonely, it's more likely to die sooner and more painfully of everything from heart attacks to cancer. In other articles, Cacioppo found that loneliness is a "public health crisis . . . that makes a person irritable, depressed, and self-centered, and is associated with a 26% increase in the risk of premature death."[28]

When your body recognizes it's lonely, the biological response is similar to being physically assaulted.[29] When people are lonely, they have overactive fight-or-flight responses[30] that cause chronic stress challenges. Having close community connections helps stave off trauma responses after devastating events.[31]

Or my favorite: the physiological cost of being lonely is greater than smoking.[32]

Loneliness is more damaging than smoking. *Let that sink in.*

How Did We Get Here?

In many ways, loneliness is baked into our cultural ethos. "My rights and my land. Get off my lawn." We kept moving west. We got higher fences. We added barbed wire. We each got our own car and our

---

28. John T. Cacioppo and Stephanie Cacioppo, "The growing problem of loneliness," *The Lancet*, February 3, 2018, https://www.thelancet.com/journals/lancet/article/PIIS0140-6736(18)30142-9/fulltext.

29. John T. Cacioppo, "The Lethality of Loneliness," TedX video, September 2013, http://www.johncacioppo.com/press/the-lethality-of-loneliness-we-now-know-how-it-can-ravage-our-body-and-brain.

30. Robert M. Sapolsky, *Why Zebras Don't Get Ulcers*, (New York: St. Martin's Press, 2004), 16.

31. Bessel van der Kolk, *The Body Keeps the Score: Brain, Mind, and Body in the Healing of Trauma*, (New York: Penguin Books, 2014), 212.

32. Cacioppo, "The Lethality of Loneliness."

own mower and our own hedge clippers. We don't borrow eggs or sugar—we just have them delivered. We shoved headphones in our ears and blocked out other voices. We went from front porches to back porches to no porches. From bars and movie theaters and churches to alcohol delivery services, streaming services, and home church in our pajamas.

We now filter our relationships through technology. We go to live concerts and watch them through our phone cameras. We don't need to navigate the delicate dance of intimacy, desire, and rejection; we've got sex, sexuality, and desire on demand. We don't need to go on grand adventures, risking failure and accomplishing harrowing goals; we can play video games with cheat codes and infinite lives. We don't need to sit in classrooms or boardrooms or neighborhood association meetings and experience the discomfort of different opinions and conclusions, the rejection of our great ideas, or the pain of being outvoted. We just learn from home, work from home, and attend Zoom meetings in our shorts.

We know more about the lives of our favorite celebrities than we do about the woman living in the apartment above us.

We're playing community.

As a result, it *looks* like we are less lonely than ever. Every friend we've ever known is on our social network. Every parent of every student is reachable by email. Every member of every church has a cell phone number. I can literally communicate with anyone on the planet.

But communication is not connection. Communication is the transfer of information. Connection is the mutual weight-bearing of one another's burdens and the celebrating of one another's joys.

We don't do that anymore.

So before we leave this section, let me be super clear and direct: Loneliness is poison. It is *literally* killing us.[33] Loneliness cripples us physically, unwinds us mentally, and makes it impossible to be spiritually whole.

The truth is, we were made for connection—for real, meaningful, in-person give-and-take with people we trust and love. We were created *as relationships.* Our bodies physically regulate themselves in relationships with others. This means that our relationships actually help us heal from trauma, physical pain, and loss, just as the *absence* of relationships *causes* trauma, physical pain, and loss.

Trust me, I don't like it either. I was born and raised in Texas, home of the Lone Ranger. I was trained to believe that I could be well all by myself. That I could only count on me. That I did not need other people.

This story is a lie.

Now What?

One of my first doctoral professors was known for asking a single, terrifying question at the end of a doctoral candidate's dissertation defense. After five or six years as a doctoral student, and after running the gauntlet of the dissertation study and defense, you'd still have to answer this professor. He would sit pensively in his chair for a moment, gathering the silence and energy in the room. Then he'd lean back, take his pen from his mouth and ask, "So what now?"

This question could feel like an insult, but it wasn't. It was an invitation. An invitation to explain why the study was important and what we were supposed to do with all this new information.

---

33. N. Leigh-Hunt et al, "An overview of systematic reviews on the public health consequences of social isolation and loneliness," *Science Direct,* November 2017, https://www.sciencedirect.com/science/article/abs/pii/S0033350617302731.

I can imagine you, the reader, asking a similar question: "Well, thanks, Delony. So what do I do now?"

Before you move to solve anything, you have to take inventory of the stories operating in your life.

Before we move on to other stories, take a few minutes to process what you've just read about your ecosystem. To do this, you have to create space between your stories and your body. A gap between your thoughts and your instant excuses and physical reactions. Jocko Willink calls it *detachment*. Michael Singer calls it *mindfulness*. My therapist friend Matt calls it *awareness*. However you label it, the result is the same. You have to create distance between your thoughts and your body.

The best way to do this is to write your stories down. Get them out of your body and onto paper. I carry a small notebook with me everywhere I go for this purpose. At the end of the next few chapters, I'll pose some questions for your reflection. Most people skip these questions—I'm asking you not to. Be brave and take a few minutes. The insights you'll discover will change your life.

Also, keep in mind that each of us is different. Some people are already debt-free. Others have already given up social media. Your stories will be unique to you. Grab a notebook to write in and answer the following questions.

Your Stories

Technology and Innovation

1. Open your phone and check out your phone usage. How often are you on your phone every day?
2. How many minutes/hours do you spend on social media, the internet, or a screen every day (including for work)?

3. Count the number of screens you see in an average day. This includes at home (phone, tablets, televisions), in your car's dashboard, at work, etc.
4. How many online accounts and passwords do you have?
5. How long has your job existed? Is it secure?

Debt

6. Calculate the ENTIRE amount of debt you are carrying. List ALL debts in order from smallest to largest. Include every single student loan, credit card, department store card, business debt, car loan, home mortgage, any rental property, etc.
7. Add all the numbers together and come up with a total debt amount.

I Don't Need Anyone but Me

8. Make a list of your five very best friends.
9. How long have you known them?
10. Name some of the tough times and good times you've shared together.
11. How often do you hang out with and/or call your friends?
12. Who would you call at 2:00 a.m. if you needed someone to come over and watch your kids?
13. When is the last time you wept in front of your friends? What was going on?
14. When is the last time you laughed so hard you almost peed in your pants with your friends?

When you're done, take a break if you need one and then keep reading.

This chapter discussed some of the stories we were born into—stories about the realities of technology, the truth of debt, and the cost of independence. In the next two chapters we'll explore two other types of stories we were born into: stories about ourselves and stories about our relationships. These stories are new frontiers in human history, and they are shaking the foundation of what whole, connected, and well living looks and feels like.

CHAPTER 4

Stories About Ourselves

Several years ago, I was part of a university leadership group that participated in a brain study. We partnered with a renowned research institute at another university to learn about the most recent advances in neuroscience. The research included my colleagues and I each taking some tests that would help us learn about our own brains and gain some tools for managing ourselves and working together as a team. Ultimately, we hoped to equip our students with new tools for managing themselves and their coursework.

We met with multiple experts and took multiple tests. It required multiple flights and a lot of meetings. Some of my colleagues were skeptical and unimpressed—I was all in. I wanted my life and my teaching to be revolutionized. I wanted to be a part of transforming university education and helping to change the way students learned about themselves, their disciplines, and their relational IQ.

When the time came to get our final "now what" reports, I was thrilled. I couldn't wait for the findings.

The brain experts flew in to present their discoveries. If I remember correctly, they had seven or so major recommendations for our collective group. As they walked us through the findings, I began feverishly taking notes. As the experts continued to reveal their recommendations, I found myself taking fewer and fewer notes.

All of their cutting-edge insights sounded vaguely familiar. I had heard this before, but I couldn't put my finger on where. I was sure I hadn't read the information in books or gotten it in a professional seminar—these findings were just making their way into the scientific literature. As I left the meeting, somewhat unimpressed, I had my lightbulb moment. I remembered where I first heard most of this revolutionary neuroscience.

From my beloved ninety-year-old grandmother.

For years my grandmother had been telling me to turn off the television (or video games) and go outside. To play with my friends (or play dominoes with her). To walk or ride my bike instead of drive. To stop eating junk. To have adventures. To read and exercise. To play a musical instrument. To pray and be part of a faith community. She'd been telling me and showing me.

Millions of dollars of research funding and equipment, a university research wing, and dozens of faculty members, test subjects, and hundreds (if not thousands) of hours . . . to come up with advice my grandmother had been espousing for decades.

And it's not that the brain researchers were wrong—they weren't. They just weren't original. Or all that cutting edge.

Remember the stories in chapter 3 about our newly adopted saviors: technology and innovation, debt and the ability to buy anything on demand, and ultimately, ourselves? These are just three of the many new saviors (including political ideologies, academic degrees, and the scientific method) that have grown out of enlightened soil.

And over the past three hundred years, as we have walked away from our tribes to save ourselves, we have run headfirst into the realities of physical limitations. We bang our heads into the likes of physiology, psychology, and biology. As we set off on our own to save ourselves, our bodies began sounding the alarms. The alarms began ringing in our bodies and then in our homes. And then they started sounding in our workplaces and neighborhoods, and now they are ringing on a global scale.

The story was, we could outsmart nature. The story was, we could avoid the rules of biology. The story was, we got smarter than our bodies.

And these new stories are driving us mad.

In this chapter, I will unpack three stories about ourselves and how we thought we could outsmart everything.

Story 4: We're Smarter Than Sleep

In the 1940s, the average American slept 7.9 hours every night.[34] Outside of a few professions, when the sun went down, people went to bed. Stores and businesses and restaurants took a break. The world went dark.

But over the past seventy-five years, we've filled our homes with lights and plugs and screens. Businesses started staying open longer and on more days of the week. Factories and transportation added a late shift and then the overnight shift. Television added *The Late Show*, and then *The Late Late Show*, and the home-shopping networks gave way to syndicated reruns, 24-hour news cycles, and movies on demand.

Sleep was officially in the way.

---

34. Jeffrey M. Jones, "In U.S., 40% Get Less Than Recommended Amount of Sleep," Gallup, December 19, 2013, https://news.gallup.com/poll/166553/less-recommended-amount-sleep.aspx.

We all began mainlining caffeine and other stimulants, and went full tilt, 24/7.

World-renowned sleep scientist and bestselling author Dr. Matthew Walker posed an extraordinary question about the importance of sleep. When viewed through an evolutionary lens, he noted how dumb and inane sleep appears. Eight hours of sleep takes us away from a full third of a day when we could be finding food, mating, or building shelter. It leaves us completely defenseless to predators and doesn't allow us to build, learn, play, or accomplish anything. Evolution should have worked sleep out of our lives, but it didn't. Sleep has remained vital to our survival.

Our bodies need sleep. It is core to who we are and how we function.

And in the 1940s, after millions of years of requiring a full night's sleep, we suddenly declared it an annoyance. Or a luxury. A burden. Or for lazy people.

In recent years, we've jammed television sets in every room, cell phones in every pocket, and video game controllers into millions and millions of hands. Instead of sleep, we "rest" by watching television and staring at our mobile devices.

We unplug by plugging in.

Sporting events, shows, concerts, church events, and dance clubs keep our heads and bodies engaged and off the pillows.

Now, long after the sun has gone down, we can just keep going. Work longer. Take classes. Eat later. Entertainment companies view sleep as a competitor[35] to their bottom line. Slogans like "I'll sleep when I'm dead" are championed by politicians and CEOs, and

---

35. In 2017, the CEO of Netflix famously said that his two chief competitors were YouTube and sleep . . . and he thought he could make inroads on sleep.

super-stimulants like coffee, energy drinks, and Adderall have been mainstreamed.

But when you're always spun up, at some point you have to come down. In addition to injecting more stimulants than ever before in the history of the world, we're also consuming more alcohol, marijuana, and other sedatives than ever before.[36] Contrary to popular belief, alcohol,[37] marijuana, and prescription sedatives disrupt key restorative sleep cycles. They may slow us down or make us unconscious, but they don't help us sleep.

In recent years, we're sleeping an average of 6.5 hours each night (6.2 hours in Japan), and the number is still falling. That's a 15–20 percent decrease in sleep, year over year, in less than a century. On most nights, 40 percent of people in the US are getting less than six hours of sleep. This is madness—and our kids are suffering as well. Tragically, our kids are getting way less sleep[38] than their developing bodies and brains need. We are torturing our children and teenagers with our combination of early start times for school, late-evening structured activities (dance, soccer, etc.), ridiculous amounts of homework, and all-hours access to video games, TV, and social media.

Why is sleep such a big deal?

Sleep impacts our cardiovascular, reproductive, and metabolic systems; our immunity; our emotional regulation and mental health; our attention span—everything. Dr. Walker says that every

---

36. Matthew Walker, PhD, *Why We Sleep: Unlocking the Power of Sleep and Dreams,* (New York: Scribner, 2017), 29–31.

37. I was deeply saddened to find that a nightly glass of wine, bourbon, or beer can devastate REM sleep.

38. Jones, Gallup.

single human function is improved or enhanced with sleep, and *every single known psychiatric disorder involves impaired sleep.*[39]

Every. Single. One.

He says that sleep is the *single most important insurance policy in the world,* our most innovative and important biohack.[40] More bluntly, Dr. Walker reports that the less a person sleeps, the more likely they are to be impacted by a whole host of diseases, including Alzheimer's, dementia, obesity, diabetes, and cancer.[41] Sleep helps balance our heart rate variability and keeps our bodies strong and connected.

Long story short: The less a person sleeps, the more likely they are to die sooner and die more painfully. This includes you.

Sleep is a giant reset button for our physical, mental, and emotional selves. It is "overnight therapy" during which our brains get power-washed from the inside out, the trash gets taken out, and our mind and body put everything back in order, ready for the next day.

Our physical bodies, our mental, spiritual, and emotional needs, and our communities and commerce have known the importance of sleep since the beginning of time. Unfortunately, those of us walking around today were born into a story that told us sleep is optional.

It's not.

Story 5: We're Smarter Than Food

Before I start this discussion, I want to be clear: when it comes to food and specialized diets, people have lost their minds. We've all gone downright mad.

---

39. Walker, *Why We Sleep,* 7.
40. Walker, *Why We Sleep,* 129.
41. Walker, *Why We Sleep,* 133, 186–187.

- I'M VEGAN and YOU'RE A MURDERER!
- Oh yeah?!!! I'm a CARNIVORE and I'M TRYING TO SAVE THE PLANET!
- Really? We'll I'm a pescatarian. Only vegetables and a little fish murder for me.
- I'm Keto. I'm raw-vegan. I only eat eggs and butter.
- I eat bugs.
- We're going to run out of food, so we need to modify everything.
- We have too much food, so we shouldn't modify anything!

Enough already.

I'm going to talk about food, so if you treat your special diet like a religion, and you're already feeling triggered, put your hand over your mouth and your cell phone down. You're a grown up and you can do hard things. Just take a deep breath and read on.

Our food is killing us.

How we consume food, what we consume, the quantities and quality of what we consume, the shaming and disordered relationships we have with food, the scientific transformation of food, the marketing around food . . . All of it.

Have you ever wondered why there are so many foods you can't say no to? Like cigarette smoking and drugs, the food industry wants to blame you, the consumer. Anything and everything you eat is your fault. Your choice. You decide.

And they're right.

Sort of.

If you eat too much junk food or if you consume too many calories, the food industry will point out that you lack willpower. You're lazy. You're too poor. You don't have enough time. You have better things to do so we prepared it for you. You need a break! You deserve a treat! This is low-fat, low-sugar, no-sugar, vegan, kosher, non-GMO, organic, and so on and so forth.

Back in the 1960s, food manufacturers started hiring a host of scientists from different fields in an effort to appeal to the whole gamut of human senses, even emotions. They used perfume experts to find the most tantalizing combinations of smells. They used visual marketers to handcraft images and choose colors that would make people feel hungry even if they weren't hungry. They called on psychologists to help them better understand the mindset behind addiction and addictive behavior.

Not to prevent it, but to weaponize it.

Job titles like chemists, marketing executives, packing architects, engineers, perfumists, and technologists make me think of building and construction, not food development.

Now make no mistake, agrarian grafting and hybrid development have been happening for millennia. Selective breeding of livestock has been going on for all of human history.

But over the past hundred years, the food we consume has been turned inside out.

Our foods have been carefully designed, constructed, and deployed to bypass our innate hunger-and-desire signaling and get us to overconsume. We've redesigned and reengineered vegetables, fruits, and grains to make them bigger, quicker, and sweeter. Our vegetables have less nutritional value than they did just a few decades ago,[42] and global soil is dangerously depleted and degraded.[43] The goal of grocers and food companies is not to satisfy hunger

---

42. Donald R. Davis, "Declining Fruit and Vegetable Nutrient Composition: What Is the Evidence?" *American Society for Horticultural Science*, February 2009, https://journals.ashs.org/hortsci/view/journals/hortsci/44/1/article-p15.xml.

43. Mark Hyman, MD, *Food Fix: How to Save Our Health, Our Economy, Our Communities, and Our Planet—One Bite at a Time*, (New York: Little, Brown Spark, 2020),

and nutritional needs. The goal is to keep you eating and eating and spending and spending.

Just the right crunch. Just the right sweet and salt. Just the right color and shape. Many of these flavor combinations are not found in nature—there is no sour cream-and-onion tree or a Dorito Taco plant or a cream-filled doughnut bush—and they overload our brain's primitive signaling responses. The food is engineered to hit different parts of your tongue at different times, and stay on your tongue just long enough for your brain to scream for the next hit.

The old Lay's potato chips slogan, "Betcha can't eat just one," wasn't a dare.

It was a promise.

My point here is that if you are trying to "eat healthy" or to learn when you're hungry or full or in need of nutrition, you're in for a fight. In some ways, it's a fight against yourself and your willpower and some nebulous idea of discipline. Holistically, you're in a fight against multitrillion-dollar industries that are hyper-focused on dictating your diet and making your nutritional decisions for you.

And you can be tough and cool and say that you don't care about farming or genetics or healthy food. That you eat what you want, when you want, and all of that. I'm not going to stop you. But know this: Almost 50 percent of Americans are considered obese—overweight enough to negatively impact their health. Three out of four Americans are pre-diabetic or dealing with metabolic syndrome.

And taxpayers are footing the bill for these choices.

But the tragedy is much bigger than economics.

Millions and millions of moms and dads can't kick a soccer ball with their kids for more than fifteen minutes. They can't ride a bike

_____

24–25, 283–284.

or go for a hike or dance into the night. They can't have sex or don't want anyone to see them naked. Metabolic disease and cardiovascular disease are real. They are painful and debilitating, and there's no bravado about it.

And don't blow me up about fat-shaming or any of that nonsense. That's not what I'm doing. I intimately know the pain and horrors associated with disordered eating, food insecurity, and special dietary needs.

I'm saying that I know your knees hurt. That your back and neck hurt. That you can't sleep. That your brain is fogged up, and that for millions of folks like me, food is a numbing agent—an addiction and a medication.

Just like the men and women in the white lab coats designed it to be.

One of the world's most powerful industries has hijacked one of our most basic primitive needs—food—then twisted it up, put some sprinkles on it, and sold it back to us.

And it's killing us.

Story 6: We're Smarter Than Death

The story of the past hundred years is that you can avoid death by outsourcing it to funeral professionals, beauticians, hospital staff, plastic surgeons, and butchers. More recently, death has been labeled a glitch in the system, not an operating rule. We've been told aging and wrinkles are largely avoidable and death soon will be. And in the meantime, any sort of direct dealing with death is largely optional, especially if you have resources.

Death has become a secret. Something we don't talk about. Taboo and hidden in the dark.

Until recently, houses and churches used to have a room

devoted to death: the *parlor*. When a person died, the body stayed in the home until the funeral, often for days. During that time, friends and family members came by to visit, family members slept in the home, and everyone was in proximity to the dead body. If you lived in the home, you went to sleep knowing the body of your husband or child or sister was a few yards away from where you were sleeping. You walked by the body on the way to the kitchen. You stepped by your loved one on the way to open the front door.

The point, of course, was to say goodbye. To accept and to grieve. To pay respects. To have a period of time where people could come to grips with the loss of someone they cared about. The parlor was connected to the practice of "sitting up with the dead"—which I know sounds morbid, but actually has psychological, spiritual, and physical healing properties. And I know there are layers to this discussion—including concerns with hygiene, disease transmission, and trauma. I'm not calling for a return to keeping the bodies of loved ones in our homes. I'm merely pointing out that what was once a normal part of the grieving process went away, virtually overnight.

Interestingly, it was 1910 when an article published in *Ladies Home Journal* officially recommended people no longer use the terms "parlor" or "death room," labeling them as echoes of the past. Can you guess what the article recommended people call that room instead?

The living room.[44] Now every home has a living room in it. There are no more parlors.

Why? A magazine fed us a story declaring death was over. A magazine told us we could just ignore it. We liked that story, it made us

---

44. Dr. Stanley B. Burns, "A Family Undertaking," PBS.org (August 3, 2004), http://archive.pov.org/afamilyundertaking/memorial-photography/.

feel less bad, and so we wallpapered over death and moved on with our lives.

Literally.

Fast forward to today, and we find a world that is increasingly allergic even to the idea of death. So we outsource it. We have funerals in funeral homes. A mortician prepares the body and stores it in a casket. A pastor delivers the eulogy. Hallmark writes our sympathy cards. A professional driver transports the body to a cemetery, and we sometimes have a viewing for an hour or two. After a short church service, a mechanical apparatus drops the body into a hole in the ground, a front loader throws the dirt back in place, and then we all go home and move on. Everything happens so quickly, for just the right price.

Our discomfort is for sale.

If we're lucky, our workplace gives us three days of bereavement leave for the death of immediate family. (We can use vacation days for cousins and grandparents.) Then it's back to work. If you're an hourly worker, well then, sucks to be you. There are financial consequences to your grief. You have to calculate how much grief you can afford. Because you still have to clock in on Friday.

And it's not just funerals either. We do our best to avoid any association with death. Most Americans have never seen an animal be killed. Few people raise and slaughter their food, and fewer people than ever fish or hunt for food. We often try to distract our kids when a pet is killed or passes away. We do anything possible to avoid death as a topic of conversation. Food appears to grow at the store.

In the same vein, even aging has become taboo. In a relatively new development, we've built entire facilities and communities for our seniors to live in. We're too busy with soccer practice and our job promotions to bother with Grandma. And our elders don't want to burden us. Grandma and Grandpa used to stay with their families until they died. In many cultures, the wisdom of the "senior" generation was revered, even when they needed taking care of. Now, we've mostly outsourced their care to others, away from the busyness of our daily lives.

On top of that, we spend billions of dollars every year pretending we're not aging—that we're not getting closer to the moment of our own death with each passing day. Lasers and fillers and plastic surgeries and teeth whitening and Botox and skin tag removal and retinol and moisturizers.

We've done everything we can think of to sanitize the concept of death, and pretend we're going to be fit, firm, and full of zeal for decades to come.

We're lying to ourselves. And to our kids.

This kind of deception always carries a cost. Even for something as inevitable and universal as death, the ground has shifted beneath us.

I remember a few years ago when my beloved ninety-four-year-old granddad passed away. He was a remarkable man. A WWII veteran, he was married to the same woman for more than seventy years, raised four remarkable kids, was a leader in his church, and was a deeply generous and invested grandparent. He even came to a few of my rock and roll shows when I was in high school. He was the best.

He died quietly, in his home, with no cancers, no strokes, and no dementia. He got up to go from one room to another, and simply passed away. He fell down dead. He slid into the afterlife with no tread left on his tires.

At his funeral, someone referred to his death as "tragic."

I miss my granddad every single day, but his death was anything but tragic. His life was a triumph and a gift, and his passing was both inevitable and beautiful. He won. And so did we.

The story is that the more we avoid death, the happier we will be. Sadly, that story is competing with a single stark truth: Death is coming for me, you, and everyone we love and care about. None of us gets out alive—and we know it.

Your Stories

As I finished writing this chapter, I felt a sense of heaviness and frustration. And these stories are just scratching the surface. There are so many more stories—like about the unimaginable rise of obesity and addiction rates across the world,[45] the untethering of faith communities in the West, and how "more than one in four American adults—and more than one in twenty American children—takes a psychiatric drug on a daily basis."[46]

I'm exhausted, annoyed, and angry at how things have become so twisted and chaotic.

It can feel like things are falling apart.

Stay with me, though.

It feels heavy, but this is not the last word. Despair doesn't win in the end.

Take a few minutes to process how these stories are at work in your life. Again, write your answers down in a notebook. This is the best way to discover what areas you need to address.

---

45. Anna Lembke, MD, *Dopamine Nation: Finding Balance in the Age of Indulgence*, (New York: Dutton, 2021), 29.
46. Lembke, *Dopamine Nation*, 38.

Take an honest inventory of your sleep.

1. How long do you sleep each night? If you track your sleep, take a rolling average of the past thirty days or so.
2. Do you have screens in your bedroom? Do you turn off screens an hour or two before bed? When you wake up in the morning, do you immediately grab your phone?
3. Do you go to bed the same time every night and get up at the same time every morning?
4. Do you eat and/or drink alcohol before bed?

Take an honest inventory of the food you eat.

5. What did you have for breakfast, lunch, dinner, and snacks this past week (as best you can remember)?
6. How much of your food comes from packages versus fresh foods?
7. What is your relationship to food? Do you eat enough? Eat too much? Have you ever struggled with disordered eating habits?
8. Do you eat to numb or avoid pain?
9. Do you cook your own food? Grow your own food?
10. What specialized diet do you follow, if any? Why do you follow it? Did you get the information about this diet from a doctor? A nutritionist? An internet influencer or social media personality? From books? *Why do you eat the way you do?*

Take an honest inventory of your relationship to death.

11. Do you have a will? (I don't care if you think you don't have enough assets for a will! You need one!)

12. Do your parents have a will and have you discussed it with them?
13. Did you grow up going to funerals? Name the last three funerals or visitations you attended.
14. When is the last time you talked about death outside of a funeral?
15. Do you hunt and/or raise your own food? When is the last time you killed something?
16. List your beauty/anti-aging procedures (and how often you do them or have them done). This includes botox, teeth whitening, hair coloring, etc.

When you're done, we've got one more chapter to go on the stories we were born into—the stories about our relationships.

CHAPTER 5

Stories About Relationships

I n 1971, my parents were married in a small ceremony. Mom was twenty and Dad was nineteen. He was in college, with two years left on his degree in Business Administration. He worked a few hours a week as a part-time security officer at the university. She was an assistant manager at a local insurance company. She did a number of jobs, including calculating agent revenues and registering the punch cards into the super computer.

My mom's job with the insurance company was enough to pay rent on their small apartment, my dad's tuition, and to generally support the two young lovebirds.

Unbelievably, she was unable to get a credit card in her name or open a checking account without my dad's name on it.

It was against the law.

Not until 1974, when Congress passed the Equal Credit Opportunity Act—a federal civil rights law—did this change. This legislation protected individuals from discrimination by banks and financial lenders, including credit companies. Such a law was necessary because it was difficult at the time for women to receive financing for home loans or small business loans, or even to open their own bank accounts. Two years later, the law was amended to criminalize lender discrimination on the basis of race, color, age, and religion.[47]

Imagine this for a moment.

When my mom and dad started dating, she wasn't allowed to get a checking account on her own. Fifty years later, she is wrapping up her final year as the chair of the English Department at a nationally recognized university, managing budgets, staff, and presenting her research all over the world.

When my dad got married, all decisions, transactions, and planning had to go through him. My mom was raised as a second-class citizen. Over the past fifty years, my dad has had to learn new relationship skills that his grandfather and great-grandfather did not know. He's had to learn to listen, submit, change his mind, say "I'm sorry," and otherwise be a co-pilot. On the other hand, my mom has had to learn about self-worth, leadership, and financial security. She has often asked why men give up their kids, spouses, and friendships *for more meetings?*

My parents' marriage is just one type of relationship that has been transformed in recent history. All types of relationships have changed. The stories informing the rules and roles of every kind of relationship, from family and kids to work and communities, look and operate differently today than they did not that long ago. The old tools and pictures don't work anymore.

Our parents and grandparents have the scars to prove it.

---

47. Federal Trade Commission, "Your Equal Credit Opportunity Rights," *Federal Trade Commission Consumer Information*, January 2013, https://www.consumer.ftc.gov/articles/0347-your-equal-credit-opportunity-rights.

We have scars too.

The basic foundation of our relationships has changed. We're lonely, exhausted, and the relational IQ we picked up from our parents and grandparents no longer serves as a successful or viable model.

We desire more from our marriages and our workplaces and our families.

We want something different from others.

We need something different from others.

We want to be different with others.

We desperately need real connection—but we're sick of the hurt, lack of boundaries, anger, and emotional and relational immaturity.

We've been fighting and running for so long . . . and now we're frozen.

As therapist and bestselling author Esther Perel says, "We just want to feel completely known."[48]

In the following pages, I've handpicked a few of the stories we've been born into about relationships, including stories about the new rules of marriage, the role of kids, the new pictures of family, and how modern friendship is broken.

Story 7: You Complete Me

In the past fifty years, the institution of marriage has undergone a transformation never before seen in the history of the world. The rules of sex, intimacy, connection, autonomy, and purpose have all

---

48. Esther Perel, *Mating in Captivity: Unlocking Erotic Intelligence*, (New York: Harper, 2006), 41.

changed—virtually overnight. Most couples have vague ideas that things aren't going well, but they can't figure out why.

I hear from couples all over the country:

- "We're not on the same page."
- "We haven't been intimate or had sex in months/years."
- "We're basically roommates."
- "We don't share money or finances and can't figure out why we're struggling so much."
- "We're getting divorced."
- "She cheated on me."
- "Pornography . . ."
- "I'm starting to have feelings for a co-worker."

What is going on?

As I noted in chapter 3, people used to live in small villages where everyone worked together to raise kids, build homes, and eat. There wasn't much of a choice in this arrangement: everyone was solving for safety and survival, and they needed one another.

All was not perfect: there were deeply entrenched social hierarchies—often faulted along gender roles—that determined who got to speak, whose ideas mattered, who got to create, and who had to do what they were told. Additionally, there were entrenched communal participation and work roles, again often divided by gender. This was sometimes based on physical qualities (women have a uterus, and as that workplace philosopher Dwight Schrute once suggested, men have strong arms), and other times it was informed by demands of the gods.

In other words, women had babies and raised kids, while men cut down trees and built homes. Women procreated; men protected. Women worked the homestead, providing food, gardening, clothes, and shelter, while men fought, hunted, scavenged, and tended to "their" domestic chores.[49]

As the Western world expanded, people spread out. *We* became *me*. *Our* community became *my* land. Tribes became families, and families ceased to be integrated communities. They fenced themselves in by blood and barbed wire.

For wealthy people, marriages were economic transactions, generally used for kingdom building, territorial expansion, or political gain. By and large, women were possessions, and marriage became a legal transaction between the father of the bride and a suitor.

You know, the classic trade of goats for girls.

For the poor, marriage was a buffer against a brutal and short life. The point wasn't to find "the one," but rather to find the "someone."

In no way was marriage for romance, intimacy, or connection. It was for property, prosperity, procreation, and protection. Of course, love, partnership, and even passionate connection existed. But those feelings were not the point.

Terrence Real says that historically, "People spoke of husbands and wives almost exclusively in terms of their roles—someone to help with the cooking and cleaning, raise the children, manage the farm. . . . Demands for connection, passion, emotional support would have been seen by most as irrelevant, even indulgent."[50]

This is how the world worked for the vast majority of human history.

And then suddenly, in the past hundred years, and especially over the past fifty years, women's voices were uncaged. Women

---

49. I know that anthropologists the world over are waving their arms wanting to talk about nuance—but generally speaking, this picture is close enough.

50. Terrence Real, *How Can I Get Through to You? Closing the Intimacy Gap Between Men and Women*, (New York: Scribner, 2002), 37–38.

entered the workforce *en masse*, took leadership roles, smashed glass ceilings, and were finally recognized for the brilliant thinkers, problem solvers, and connected beings they are. We quickly upscaled an economic model that required two incomes per household to stay afloat. There was more economic mobility and opportunity. More access to capital, more freedom to do whatever women wanted to do.

They started leaning into what they felt like doing instead of what they were told they had to do.

Esther Perel calls this "a period of unmatched freedom and individualism."[51] Suddenly there were no more rules. Or very few rules that mattered. And our brains, bodies, and spirits have yet to catch up.

Divorce became quick and easy, just another contractual transaction. Don't like your spouse? Get a new one. And though we are still a long way from equity, women gained newfound economic freedom to leave, start again, move, and demand that workplaces take their needs into account.

Just like men have always been able to.

We used to have duty, obligations, geographical limitations, or religious or cultural expectations because we needed these institutions to keep us alive.

No more.

Now every one of us can do whatever we want, all by ourselves.

And we call this freedom.

But as Perel notes,

Trailing in the shadow of this manifest extravagance lies a new kind of gnawing insecurity. The extended family, the

---

51. Perel, *Mating in Captivity*, 8.

community, the religion may indeed have limited our freedom . . . but in return they offered us a much-needed sense
of belonging. For generations, these traditional institutions
provided order, meaning, continuity, and social support.
Dismantling them has left us with more choices and fewer
restrictions than ever. We are freer, but also more alone . . .
Modern life has deprived us of our traditional resources,
and has created a situation in which we turn to one person
for the protection and emotional connections that a multi-
tude of social networks used to provide. Adult intimacy has
become overburdened with expectations.[52]

Our grandparents (and their parents before them, and so on
back through history) became "soulmates" after thirty or forty or fifty
years in the trenches together. They fell deeply in love through shared
experience and common goals. Love was a byproduct of stability.

My generation (and younger) is trying to find their soulmate
first, and then reverse-engineer a meaningful life around our feelings. We start with *You complete me* and work backwards.

We are trying to run the relational algorithm in reverse, and it's
failing.

Please don't miss how important this transformation truly is.
Women fought and the rules changed. The rules changed for men,
but they didn't know what to do next. Marriages changed from economic arrangements, political transactions, or teams of procreat-
ing survivors—to *You complete me.*

Where I used to turn to entire religious, community, and trade
connections for help, support, esteem, and existential value—I now
just turn to my spouse. And she to me.

---

52. Perel, *Mating in Captivity*, 8–9.

That is too much for one person to carry. We've set each other on fire for warmth and it's not going well.

So we plod along, using the same pictures of marriage and intimacy that we learned from our parents, all while yearning for marriages that are recklessly intimate, alive, and fulfilling. We run households and raise children together, but we fantasize in digital wastelands. We're roommates and co-managers.

But we want more.

Story 8: The World Revolves Around the Kids

When we dissolved our tribes, we became all about families. Blood. Here in the US, we moved west, had a million kids to work our farms, and assumed a number of them would not survive the journey. Infant mortality was high. Then we moved to cities. Or we threw up cities in former agricultural trading hubs. We moved into air-conditioned homes. Healthcare improved dramatically. And as we stopped needing kids to assure our survival, our kids took on something more sinister: they became our identity.

Our kids became trophies for us to display to the world how good we are at parenting.

Kids became a trinket; a way to silently signal how much money we have (in the form of clothes, shoes, and private school tuition); our superior genetic lines (through travel sports teams); and how we have it all together (through matching outfits and restaurant behavior).

Our kids became our reason for being.

Parents now prove their worth to the world by having successful kids. Worth shows up in a son or daughter's grades, athletic performance, music or theater performance, church attendance (and behavior), and 4-H.

Suddenly, our lives became all about our children. Are they okay? Are they sad? Do they have special needs? Are they winning? How are their grades? How fast can they throw? What percentile are they in? How tall? How fat? How skinny? Can they tumble? Twirl? Tweet? Are they dominating Fortnite?

As adults, all of our conversations are about our children. What school is your kid going too? Did they get into that college? That teacher is the worst. I don't let my kid hang out with that kid.

And with every bump and bruise along the way, there is always a new expert to tell us about a new diagnosis, a new strategy, or a new device that would give our kids the best of the best of the best. Or a new reason why our kid is different, unique, or more special than your kid. Oh, or a new prescription. We love pills.

Almost overnight, parents mortgaged their self-worth and their bank accounts to the achievements of children. *Who we are* became tied up in *how they did.*

Our ambitions, desires, and wishes are carried on the backs of our five-year-olds.

What an unfair and tragic turn of events.

Three-year-olds and seventeen-year-olds are not mature enough to carry the weight of our hopes and dreams. We must recognize that if children are not old enough to drink or buy lottery tickets, they most certainly do not have the strength and wisdom to carry our self-esteem, frustrations, and failures.

And here's something else. In the past thirty years, we parents have taken advantage of our children and co-opted them into being our friends. To be among our closest *peer relationships.* We don't have the skills to develop or maintain adult relationships, so we've invited our children into our adult lives. Into our jokes, our entertainment, our fears, and our intimate relationships. We have given our kids permission to hurt our feelings. To break our hearts. We are obsessed with making sure our kids *like us*. We're scared if they don't—we can't handle that type of rejection.

The truth is, children should never be forced to carry the weight of an adult friendship or their parents' feelings or regrets. That is not their job.

Story 9: The Changing Picture of Family

In ancient times, families were made up of cousins, parents, kids, the elderly, and the neighborly. This was the picture of families for thousands of years. But as we noted above, as the world expanded west, our place became "my" place. "Leave and cleave" grew to mean "mine and y'alls."[53]

Within the last century, our culture invented a picture of the modern family that was limited to two adults, 2.3 kids, and a dog. Two cars. Two jobs. One picket fence. Lots of smiles. No friction. Pictures of these families took over movies, TV shows, articles, and books.

This meant anyone who found themselves in a home with divorced parents was broken. Anyone who struggled with infertility and couldn't have kids, or who simply didn't want kids, was dysfunctional. Kids growing up in homes with two moms or two dads, as a family of five living in a one-bedroom apartment, or where both sets of grandparents lived with you, felt like oddballs.

You can see the problem with this story. You may even have *lived* the problem.

For a long time now, there have been many families that look very different from what culture says is "normal." I'm talking about

---

53. I know, I know. This is only a word in Texas.

biracial families. Families impacted by divorce. Blended families. Foster families. Gay and lesbian families. Families that have adopted children. Families led by single parents. Families with kids with special needs.

People start asking why our kids aren't married when they reach the age of twenty-five. Or they ask us how we could even allow our kids to be thinking of marriage at the age of twenty-five. Some folks are disgusted by parents who leave their kids at daycare. Other folks are disturbed by the idea of stay-at-home-parents. A friend of mine who is a brilliant law scholar and a remarkable wife, mother, and friend, told me that she was once called a "breeder" by some of her colleagues—as though the idea of having kids meant she was not as invested in her career as she otherwise could be. Having a family can be a professional liability, and not having one can also be a professional problem.

It doesn't matter whether you agree or disagree or like or dislike all the different pictures of families. The truth is that a single, unified picture of the "normal" family no longer exists.

Yet the stories surrounding the picture of families have become a battleground. There are many voices telling us what a family is supposed to look like. Loud and angry voices. Voices saying we need to return to a "traditional" picture—the 2.3 kids and the two cars and all of that—while others say we need to burn the traditional picture to ashes.

In between the yelling and the fighting, most folks are trying to do the best they can with the cards they've been dealt.

We were all born into stories of what family is and what family should look like. And some folks live something similar to that picture. But for millions and millions of others, the story of family is an evolving one, built on a foundation of love, circumstance, and making do.

Story 10: Digital Relationships Complete Me

About a decade ago, I was teaching an undergraduate seminar course to about eighty sophomores and juniors. Smartphones, tablets, and social media had just been released to the wild and, overnight, human communication went digital. I came up with an educational exercise to show my students just how much the roles and rules of friendship had changed.

I broke the class up into small groups and sent them out into the local community. Their task was a simple one: They had to recreate social media relationships in the real world. They had to meet and interact with people in real life, using the new rules of social media communication. My ground rules for the assignment were (1) that they couldn't preface the interactions with "This is a class assignment," and (2) they had to engage the interactions with a straight face. They couldn't give away the punchline.

The exchanges went something like this:

Students (walking in a group toward a stranger in a mall): "Excuse me, sir!"

Stranger (looking around and awkwardly shifting bags of clothes): "Uhh, yeah? Me?"

Students: "Yes! You. I was walking by, saw you, and wondered: Will you be my friend? Can I see pictures of your family? What are your political preferences? Can I see the pictures of your tattoos? What are your religious preferences? Why? Are you pro-choice? How come? Who are your favorite musicians? We're going to read you a list of probing, introspective quotes, and you simply give us a thumbs up or a thumbs down if you like them or don't like them. If you feel angry about a quote, tell us why."

And so on.

My students had to video each interaction. And yes, it was as awkward and cringey as you can imagine. According to the papers they had to write after the fact, the assignment stirred up quite a bit of reflection.

In a few short years, my students had come to believe they had "friends" because *they knew some information about people.* They thought they were connecting with those people. The exercise helped them see that our social media exchanges are anything but normal. The thumbs ups and thumbs downs are anything but connecting.

The reality is that most of us don't have any friends.

Until recently, friendship was about enduring the awkwardness and ugliness of human interaction and choosing to remain anyway. Two hundred years ago, friends looked out for your family and plowed your fields when you were injured. When I was writing my dissertations, friends brought pizza and Dr Pepper to my wife after the third week in a row of her having to do kids' bedtimes by herself. My friend sat with me in the hospital while the doctors performed emergency surgery on my wife, trying to save both her and our unborn baby. She made it and the baby did not. In the old days, that's what people did for each other. Friends ran to other cities to check on their friends. They made meals with their hands and delivered them with their feet. They wrote handwritten letters, licked the stamp, and sent them.

Friends hung out in person. Friends disagreed in person and let the weight of the disagreement hang in the air. It was uncomfortable and tense—but no one ever questioned whether they'd show up again tomorrow. Friends put up with your weirdness and you always being late, and you put up with theirs. They told you everything and loved you anyway. And you loved them.

Friendships were everything.

In this new century, most of our friends have been shoved into fancy digital boxes with 3- or 4-inch screens. We've traded quality for quantity, and we're drowning in shallow water.

I recently talked with a caller on my show named Sydney who was mourning the lack of a social support system. She and her husband had moved away from family a couple years back, and their jobs didn't really allow for making new friends. Then came the Covid-19 pandemic, and the isolation she was feeling suddenly became much, much worse.

"I'm sure you can understand that having some online friends is good," Sydney told me, "but it's not the same as having someone over for coffee." She wanted some advice on how to make "real-life friends."

"Real-life" is now a distinguishing characteristic.

Social media has redefined the word *friend* for us. Now "friend" means curated people who report liking the things they think you like and hating the things they think you hate. It means engaging with you on their terms and dipping in and out as they feel compelled. Comparing, sharing, and judging without the weight in the room.

One of the most important relationships in the world was transformed by a tech company.

And it happened overnight.

Now before you close this book and feed it to Alexa—I know there are meaningful and real interactions that take place online. Research tells us that people are more likely to divulge truths, share, and interact online. People spill their guts and vomit their feelings, and these interactions feel deep and transformative.

They kind of are . . . and they kind of aren't. Being honest and vomiting up feelings are important, but they should not be the highwater mark for friendship.

Presence is. Showing up is. Being fully known and still fully loved is.

Hitting the "thumbs up" emoji is not friendship. Laying down your life is.

I moved to a new city in a new state several years ago, so I get it. I'm super slow to trust and I know firsthand: making new friends is hard. I'm still trying to figure it out. It's uncomfortable and messy, especially for adults. It's easier to just text and send memes to my old friends. And there's nothing wrong with that.

But it's not a substitute.

The story that digital friends is equivalent to—or even an upgraded version of—"real-life" friends is tragically mistaken.

Your Stories

Our stories of the role and function of marriage, our kids, our families, and our friendships are changing and churning by the moment. In some cases, the stories have changed so dramatically in such a short period of time that it will take years to understand the implications.

Take a few minutes now to think about how these stories impact your life and write down your responses in your notebook.

Marriage

1. If you're married, why did you get married? If you're not married, what concerns or stories might be holding you back from choosing to get married?
2. Are you in a serious, long-term relationship? Why are you in this relationship?
3. How do you and your significant other make decisions in your relationship? Who gets the final say?

4. Name three to five ways you honor your romantic partner every single day. Name three to five ways they honor you every single day.
5. Name three things you love about your current romantic relationship.
6. Name three things you would love to change about your current relationship.

Parenting

7. How many children do you have?
8. What is the ratio of time spent on caring for yourself and your romantic relationship, versus the amount of time spent on your kids. Be specific.
9. How many children's events/rehearsals/practices/birthday parties/playdates did you attend over the past thirty days?
10. How many of your conversations with your romantic partner involve your kids?
11. Have you ever said the words "I'm best friends with my son/daughter."

Your Picture of Family

12. How many parents/grandparents live with you?
13. How many divorces, single parents, foster children, and adopted children are in your immediate family?
14. How many brothers and sisters do you have? Where do they live? What do they do for a living?
15. How often do you see and/or interact with your immediate family? Your extended family (cousins, aunts, uncles)?

Digital Relationships

16. How many people do you have as "friends" on your online media accounts (including LinkedIn, Facebook, Instagram, etc.)?
17. What is the ratio between online "friends" and real-world friends?
18. How often do you play online games or watch streaming events remotely with "friends"?
19. What's the ratio of digital interactions with "friends" and in-person interactions with friends, church people, and family?
20. What's the ratio of games, concerts, and talks you watch online versus attend in person?

We've been looking at the stories we're born into. These come largely from culture and are familiar to us regardless of the impact they've had on us.

Next, we're going to look at two other types of stories that operate in our lives: the stories you've been told and the stories that actually happened. These stories are different because they don't come to us from the wider culture, but from the people in our lives.

CHAPTER 6

Stories We're Told and That Happened

I n second grade, my teacher, Ms. Mosley, assigned our class a two-page writing assignment. We were to write a mini-research paper about something we loved, drafted on tall, one-inch-lined handwriting paper. I had just seen the latest *Karate Kid* movie, and I was crane-kicking everyone and waxing on-and-off everything. Naturally, I wrote my paper on karate. I'd seen the movies and now I considered myself a karate expert. I began writing with fervor. I blew past the first two pages and kept on cranking. I was in flow.[54]

After a few days of me tuning out the rest of the class for the sake of this paper, Ms. Mosley let me move my chair to the back of the room during our literacy and writing time just so I could keep writing.[55] I became entranced with the idea that I was a writer, a karate expert, and a creator. I was making a "new thing" on that lined paper. I was telling stories.

---

54. Mihaly Csikszentmihalyi, *Flow: The Psychology of Optimal Experience*, (New York: Harper Perennial, 1990), 4.

55. I now realize that a busy and engaged John was a quiet and somewhat still John, which made for a better learning environment for everyone . . . but whatever.

I ended up with a good grade on the assignment. But more importantly, while Ms. Mosley was walking up and down the classroom rows, handing back our papers, she gave me a powerful affirmation far beyond a simple red-inked check +. As she handed me my paper, she bent down and said, "Wonderful job, John. You have a great imagination and you're an excellent writer."

And then she just kept walking.

I showed my mom and dad my research assignment/karate story. They told me—and showed me—how proud they were. My mom sent a few copies to extended family members, and a few of my uncles mentioned the assignment during the holidays. Even my older sister told me "Good job." She was the smartest person I'd ever met, and I craved her affirmation. (I still do.)

Fast-forward more than three decades, and I now write and tell stories for a living. I speak to millions of radio and podcast listeners every month. I use my imagination and experience to connect a diverse array of academic disciplines and personal challenges to give people hope and direction. Even when I was a leader in universities, I was always writing opinions and reports, and using stories to teach my students and lead my teams.

Ms. Mosely gave me a new story, which became an identity. My family affirmed the story. From passing comments to hugs and high-fives, I was encouraged about my ability to write and communicate. This story continues to impact me to this day.

I am a good writer. I am a good storyteller. I have a good imagination.

In chapters 3, 4, and 5 we explored the stories we're born into. These stories are the air we breathe, and they come to us from our ecosystem. In this chapter, we're going to explore the stories we're told by others.

These stories are powerful guides for our lives. They shape our interests and identity, direct our talents, and influence the people and careers we pursue.

As you read this chapter, keep in mind the stories others tell us are both positive and negative. Benign and malignant. Strangely, some stories bounce off us like Teflon, with little to no impact. Other stories lodge themselves into our hearts and our DNA, altering how we see and approach the world.

And these stories aren't just about things that happened to us as children. They also include ten years ago, two weeks ago, and this morning. Whether you like it or not, these stories play a role in the person you are right now.

The Stories Told by Others

Mom. Dad. Step-parent. Grandma. Grandpa. Brother. Sister. Neighbor. Pastor. School pals. School bullies. The people at your church and in your neighborhood. Your favorite—or most hated—politician. The abuser. The coach or teacher. The mechanic. The motivational influencer or the former Navy Seal who pumps you up on social media. The kind woman at the Starbucks register or the jerk at the box-store counter. Or even that anonymous stranger who sends you uplifting messages on social media.

From the day we're born, many people have access to our lives—specifically our minds, hearts, and bodies—and they tell us stories. We often think of access as something physical, like touch or proximity. But access more often includes verbal and visual connections. Access to hearts and minds and ears and eyes. Stories are told through media, through teaching, through snippet interactions.

Some of these stories are empirically true and factual, and we know it: How tall we are. How big (or small) our noses are. How well our pants fit. How well we read or pass math tests. How old our car is. How much money we have in the bank or how fast we can run a mile.

Yet importantly, many stories we're told are *not* true. Or they're partially true. Some stories are not real or correct or appropriate. For instance, someone tells you to lose some weight—but you have no weight to lose. Someone might look at your standardized test scores or your lack of a graduate degree and tell you that you're not smart, but maybe you weren't a good test taker. Or you might have been living in an unsafe, chaotic environment that made concentration on *any* test very difficult.

Regardless of how true those stories may or may not be, they impact our lives. They change us. They create us. They generate drive or collapse motivation. The stories we're told about who we are and what we're capable of create the invisible (or sometimes not-so-invisible) brick walls of our world. They impact how our genes turn on and off in various situations, whether we see obstacles as opportunities or catastrophes, and how we form or avoid intimate relationships. These stories inspire us to overcome or encourage us to hide.

You may have heard the saying that your childhood biography becomes your adult biology. This is true. The stories you're told by others impact you in physiological and biochemical ways. Here's an example of how story impacts your body:

Imagine you are fourteen years old.

You've got a big test coming up in your geometry class. Your dad let you know that any kid who fails a math test is either stupid, incapable, or lazy. Or maybe all three. He's trying to motivate you and communicate that no kid of his will be stupid or lazy. Your mom says nothing, affirming his rants with her silence.

Your dad is strong, and you assume he's smart, so you trust him. Like most kids, you trust him more than you trust yourself. And of course, you trust your mom.

You need to pass this test.

You've learned in the past that your grades have power. One time you bombed a reading quiz in your boring language arts class. You earned an *F*. Your parents saw your grade and yelled at you. Or shook their heads in silent disappointment and disgust. They said you made them sad. Or they wouldn't talk with you. Or your grade "made" them drink. Or they hit you "for your own good."

You see the other kids in your class who get good grades and you fantasize about their parents' reactions—how proud they must be. Your stomach feels heavy like lead and your head feels dull. Your breaths are shallow. Your body acknowledges you are all alone. After all, your exam scores control the feelings and actions of the grown-ups in your life, and you—the fourteen-year-old—are responsible for harnessing and wielding that power.

Now imagine your body gearing up for fighting, running, or hiding as your teacher walks the rows, handing out the geometry exams. Your performance on this exam will impact the attitude of the adults in your home. It may impact your safety. It will certainly impact your social life and your connectivity to your community. You've studied as well as you know how, with one eye on the material and one eye focusing on remaining safe.

Next, imagine your body seizing up as your teacher hands back the graded exams. Your heart is racing and your stomach is in your feet. You may have a headache or one side of your neck feels tight. When your teacher hands you the paper and you see the RED *F* in the top right-hand corner of the page,

BOOM! Your brain and body fire on all cylinders.

Before you can even cognitively process what's happening, your body is off to the races, trying to protect you from what happens next. Your brain quickly puts 1 + 1 together: You got the *F* and your parents will be so disgusted that they can't look at you. YOU made them angry = their response is *your* fault! And since the brain works on ancient technology, it assumes that if a child gets left by their parents, it means certain death. If our caregivers leave us, we will starve or have no defense against wolves or bears or warring neighbors. So your brain will do everything it can to solve the broken relationship.

Your body senses danger, dumping cortisol and adrenaline into your bloodstream to prepare for the fight or the sprint to safety. It uptakes any and all available glucose from your bloodstream and triggers an increase in neurotransmitters and neuromodulators,[56] all to sharpen your senses and increase awareness of physical and relational needs. Your body will need extra strength to survive what's coming from Mom and Dad. Either strength to absorb your physical punishment, or wit, charm, and focus to blame your teacher or the test, or to help you reconnect.

For a child, disconnection from their parents means death.

What can you do to fix this? How can you be seen? How can you earn back this love? How can you convince these adults in your life that you are worth feeding, hugging, and protecting? Your brain knows that you might get a brutal spanking, grounded, or exiled from your friends and gaming systems. Your body is simply trying to survive this incident *and* protect yourself in the future.

Cue the fighting, the running, or the freezing.[57]

---

56. If you want to learn more about gene expressions, the biochemical and physiological relationships to thoughts and social standing, don't forget about the reading list at the end of this book.

57. Or in some cases, the fawning.

Some teenagers buck authority or bully other kids (fight). Others run away or turn to numbing agents like sex, drugs, or alcohol (flight). Still others shut down and withdraw, hiding under headphones, blankets, makeup, sports uniforms, or food (freeze). After the initial incident, the stories begin to impact day-to-day decisions. Each of these decisions stack up on one another.

Do you commit your life to your grades, forgoing fun and other activities for a single-minded pursuit of academic perfection? Do you assume that you can never earn affection in the classroom so you abandon it altogether and seek attention and affirmation on an athletic field, in the church youth group, or by your appearance? Do you try to be seen and heard by following destructive impulses—getting in trouble, dangerous behaviors, or seeking thrills? Does your body develop real medical challenges that inspire empathy from school officials, medical personnel, and your caregivers?

Notice we haven't even asked if the original stories are true. It doesn't matter if parents are well-meaning, well-trained, or want what is best for their children. What matters is that the stories Mom and Dad live out—the yelling, hitting, ignoring, the disgust or the overreaction—cause real and true physical reactions in the body of the fourteen-year-old.

Over time, as your body reacts with a full fight-or-flight response, it craves the chemicals spun up by school exams. You become addicted to the chemicals. For your adolescent brain, a simple geometry test has become a relational minefield of extraordinary stakes. A place to prove worthiness, value, and lovability. And it has become a chemical cocktail and neural roadmap of stimulus, response, and reward. Our minds automate these responses and they continue to run in the background, spinning us up and crashing us down over and over again. The responses imprint and inform future responses in related situations.

Ten years later, when your boss sends back your report that she's not happy with, your body spins up again.

Seventeen years later, when your wife tells you she's unhappy in your marriage because you're not living up to her expectations, your body remembers the drill.

Twenty-five years later, when your son tells you he hates you, your body remembers.

It remembers this "fire drill."

And this is just one story.

Our brains never stop. They're always scanning the environment for negative stories and for the worst possible outcomes. For places where we don't belong. For people and threats that could hurt us. Looking for threats is how we stay alive: Our brain's goal is not thriving. Its goal is not dying.

So we take in the messages and stories from caregivers, teachers, coaches, pastors, entertainers, politicians, babysitters, peers, and strangers over time, and we end up fighting or running from everyone and everything. Or running to people who don't have our best interest in mind. Or our body says, "I can't do this anymore," and it just freezes.

It's the stories.

The stories we were told—and are told—deeply impact our bodies.

The Truth About the Stories Others Tell Us

Here are a few important truths about the stories others tell us.

The stories others tell us often have nothing at all to do with us. Mom yells about your grades because she is professionally limited by her academic shortcomings. Or that's her way of saying "I love you" or "I'm trying to keep you safe." Or Dad calls you fat because of his lifelong challenges with his weight, and because of the bullying he endured from friends and family. Or because he wants the world to see how beautiful you really are, and he only knows one way to motivate you.

Stories come with all sorts of baggage, with all sorts of intentions, and with all sorts of meanings. Don't miss this: *stories for us and about us are sometimes not for us or about us.*

The stories we're told are both explicit and implicit. Someone can tell you that they hate you, or they can just ignore you.

Explicit stories are direct. Think of the mom who tells her daughter her hair is too curly or the coach who tells a child, "You sure have a big belly for your age."[58] Or the teacher who keeps calling out the little boy in the third row for fidgeting during class, or who tells the girls that they should sit quietly and be peacemakers.

Implicit stories are stories told *without* words. These stories may or may not be as direct, but they can still have a huge impact because the listener creates their own meaning.

Implicit stories are when you're the little Jewish kid who only sees Christmas trees and you believe your holidays and religion are less than. Or when your mom won't put down her cell phone even though you're talking to her, or when you're the only person of color in your office.

All of those are stories with impact, and all of them are stories told without words.

The stories we're told go largely unchallenged and unchecked. We accept them as true and move through life accordingly. They

---

58. It's no wonder so many kids spend the rest of their lives trying to solve for problems of appearance. They crave approval and connection, and since the adult in their world has pointed out a physical target for disconnection, the child's body will be about solving that problem.

circulate through our hearts—literally in our body chemistry and in our brains, as we've seen—and help determine the roads of life we travel on. Our bodies often react to keep us safe without our heads knowing it. Even if our frontal lobes know that we aren't fat, our bodies can begin circulating the shame/fear/flight chemicals. And we never stop to examine what's happening.

The stories we're told stack up. They form a complex matrix of feelings, assumptions, and he said-she said. Often people tell us one story and, because of other stories we've been told before, we hear something totally different. For instance, an abusive father may raise his voice as a warning that a beating is on its way. Conversely, a high school football coach may raise his voice to get your attention over the noise at practice and to communicate that you are worthy of receiving correction so that your performance can improve. But your body has a built-in response for yelling, and it is to shrink away, hide, and prepare for the beating.

It doesn't matter what your coach *meant* ... your body is already off to the races, having stacked enough stories to know that a raised voice means pain and disconnection.

The stories we're told have both rough sides and smooth sides. Blessings and curses. Lots of the stories have passed along multiple messages to you, sending you all over the place.

Ms. Mosley told me I was imaginative, good at writing, and good at storytelling. Being a "storyteller" became my calling card and my escape—and I took it way, way too far. I spent years making up stories out of fear that I wasn't cool enough or fun enough or that the truth wasn't edgy enough. Stories got me A's. Stories got me on stages and won me kudos from the adults in my life. And when I didn't have real stories to pass along, I stretched and reached and embellished.

Being a good storyteller in some situations earned me praise. In other situations, being a storyteller made me a liar.

The stories we're told can be passed along by a single voice or many voices. A community can tell you you're the wrong color and you don't belong without using any words—by assuming you're guilty before hearing your side of the story, for example, or by making sure none of the pictures, art, or food looks like anything you're comfortable with.

A company can tell important stories about a woman's worth by paying her less than similarly credentialed and experienced men doing the same job. Or by their health insurance policies, leave policies, or leadership investment and training opportunities. Companies tell us stories about how we need their products. How we won't find a girlfriend if we don't wear the right deodorant.

And social media. Social media curates and injects targeted stories about how we aren't pretty enough, good enough, popular enough, wealthy enough, or disciplined enough. As Dr. Robert Sapolsky points out,

> Thanks to urbanization, mobility, and the media that makes for a global village, something absolutely unprecedented can now occur—we can now be made to feel poor, or poorly about ourselves, by people we don't even know. You can feel impoverished by the clothes of someone you pass in a midtown crowd, by the unseen driver of a new car on the freeway, by Bill Gates on the evening news, even by a fictional character in a movie. Our perceived socio-economic status may arise mostly out of our local community, but our modern world makes it possible to have our noses rubbed in it by a local community that stretches around the globe.[59]

---

59. Sapolsky, *Why Zebras Don't Get Ulcers*, 376–377.

The stories we're told even include stories about our stories. We're told that our feelings or experiences are wrong, misguided, or stupid. That if we feel less-than, it's our fault. We're also told that reality and facts are more important than our experience or our feelings about something. Interestingly, these final two points are somewhat true, in the right context. But on their face, they still hurt.

The gaslights burn brightly.

As you think about the stories in your own life, watch for how these truths play out. And always remember that stories can be true, untrue, or partially true. That's why you have to examine each one: to see if it's helping you or harming you.

The Stories of Things We Did

Before we move on, there's another dimension to this that needs our attention. So far we've looked at the stories we've been given—from culture, from companies and social media, and from other people. We had nothing to do with these stories. They happened *to* us. But that isn't always the case.

In addition to the stories we've been told, we also need to be mindful of the stories of the things *we* did. When talking about our pain or success, we often leave that part out.

A few weeks ago, my daughter Josephine came into the house, crying from the depths of her soul. She ran into my arms, and I warmly hugged her. "What happened?" I asked, looking her over for a rattlesnake bite.

She choked/cried/talked in that lovable yet incomprehensible way, until she was finally able to catch her breath and speak clearly: "Hank hit me with a stick!"

Hank is my son and her brother.

"Why did Hank hit you with a stick?" My blood was heating up. No one hits my daughter with a stick.

"He was mad, and he just ran over and hit me for no reason," she responded.

Just then, Hank came be-bopping into the house, acting like he didn't have a care in the world.

"Did you hit my daughter in the face with a stick?" I demanded, still hugging my hurting little girl.

"Yes," Hank said, "but two things. One, she ran by me and hit me in the head with a stick. Literally for no reason. I didn't respond and instead chose to ignore her. Two, she then challenged me to a sword fight. We were fighting and I accidentally missed her stick and whopped her in the head."

Oh.

The "I hit him in the face with a stick" and "we were playing a sword-fighting game" details changed the story rather dramatically. Josephine left out the parts where she started the whole thing—and where what happened was really an accident.

Here's the hard reality that we don't like to discuss: Sometimes my pain is *my* fault.

It is a result of my poor choices. Something *I* did. Something I'm doing. And it doesn't matter why I did them—it only matters that I did them.

You drove drunk because you thought you could make it home. You sexted a picture of yourself to someone other than your spouse because you didn't think you'd get caught. You cheated on that exam. You yell at your wife.

My friend Melissa bought a new car and didn't know to change the oil. She is a brilliant professor in a medical program, has a graduate degree, two wonderful kids, a husband, and a beautiful home. But she didn't change the oil in her car. Ever. She said she was just waiting for the light to come on. And her car engine melted together. Hilarious to her friends . . . not so much to her.

She did it.

In order to heal from the stories you've been living, you have to tell yourself the honest truth about the role you've played in your current circumstances.

I screw up on a regular basis. We all do.

We make poor choices and uninformed decisions. We sign our names to loan documents, we hold grudges, we seek to make ourselves well through codependency. We tell our kids that they made us angry or sad instead of recognizing that we chose to get angry or sad. We pick at and poke and prod people. We fire off emails. We hit someone's door in the parking lot. We're late all the time. We listen to YouTubers instead of experts.

We violate boundaries. We don't show up. We turn in subpar work. We gossip at work.

Or we save the day. We change our neighbor's tire. We apologize to our kids. We love first and don't yell.

This can be a strange realization when it comes to our stories: The pain and joy we experience doesn't only come from other people. Much of our pain and joy is a result of our own choices. Yes, we're born into stories and we've been told stories. But that's not the whole picture.

This is where the truth gets hard.

You were abused. Neglected. Heartbroken. Yelled at. Born with genetic tendencies. Your parents didn't stay together. Your church was hateful and disrupting. Your boss didn't encourage you to go back to college.

All of that is true.

And you have the power to not yell at your kids. To be present with your spouse. To lean into the healing and stop the cycles of addiction, control, and abuse. You can choose to get the help you need so that you can learn how to forgive yourself, to feel your feelings, and then go make different choices. You can choose to continue showing those you lead and love that you care about them.

In chapters 3 and 4, we saw how the world has transformed right underneath our feet in sweeping and dramatic ways. You eat things you know are unhealthy because you crave them. You don't get enough sleep because you'd rather watch a couple more shows on Netflix than make the tough choice to turn off the TV. You're drowning in debt because you signed your name on that school loan.

All of that is true. *And*, you ultimately decide what you do each day.

In chapter 5, we looked at some of the many ways relationships are different and messy and mismatched. Our culture has pushed a lot of pictures on us about what families are supposed to look like. We're living in a society that constantly shouts that your spouse must be your very best friend, your financial advisor, your sexual fantasy, and your psychologist.

All of that is true. *And*, the common denominator in all of your relationships is . . . drumroll, please . . .

You.

There were times you contributed to the chaos of your family, both now and in the past. If there are problems in your relationships, then you are probably part of those problems—your choices and your expectations, your lack of boundaries or self-worth, your unwillingness to stand up for yourself, or maybe your selfishness. And if you've spent years trying to find meaning or purpose through tweets and followers, or even through your career, then you've spent years ignoring the truth in your own heart that your search wasn't working. Not by a long shot.

In this chapter we've talked about the words and actions of others that have shaped our identity in profound ways. They told us things about who we are—sometimes true and sometimes not true—and we believed them.

That's all true too. We've got the scars to prove it. *And*, it's ultimately your responsibility to examine each story and decide what to do with it.

I hope you know I'm speaking from a whole lot of experience. I'm speaking from a lifetime of bad choices, bad finances, bad relationships, and bad patterns.

Just like you, I'm doing the best I can to take a step back and figure out what went wrong—what's still going wrong—and be honest about what stories I'm still living. It's a choice.

You choose not to raise hell and to do *whatever* it takes to get out of debt. To change your living arrangement. To fix your marriage (or leave your marriage). To quit taking his money. To lose weight. To set boundaries with your family. To get a new job.

Or you choose *not* to do these things.

Face it, the ecosystems of blame, finger pointing, and finding someone else to hate will never solve your problems. They will prolong them. They will fill your body and mind with rage, or depression, or frustration, or inflammation and immobility.

I stole and lied a lot as a kid. I violated the trust of my friends. I took the wrong job. I didn't show up as a husband when I should have. I told too many jokes that were not only *not* funny but also downright marginalizing and heartbreaking. I took on six-figures of student loan debt. I've done things I shouldn't.

I. Did. Those. Things.

Part of healing is owning what you've done. You welcome accountability. You accept the truth. It takes courage to admit your part, but doing so is how you take a step toward freedom and a new way of life.

It is about acknowledging reality.

This is the only way forward.

Your Stories

Once again, set aside some time to begin reflecting on the stories you were told and the stories that actually happened. Here are some questions to get you started:

1. What is the story of your body? Who told you that you were beautiful? Not beautiful? Handsome? Overweight? Too skinny?
    - Were you abused? Forced to kiss aunts and uncles you didn't want to be close to?
    - Were you loved and taken care of?
    - What did your caregivers say about their bodies? Were they always on a diet? Did they exercise? Were they overweight? Did they have chronic pain?
2. What is the story of your intelligence? Who told you that you were smart? Or that you were dumb? Or that they expected you to get straight A's in school?
    - Were there books in your home growing up?
    - Did your parents or caregivers read to themselves or read to you?
3. Did you feel valued? Were you ignored? Were you doted on? Did your parents or caregivers have high expectations of you? Or were they passive?
4. Were you allowed to be you, or were you told you were too emotional, sensitive, loud, or silly?

5. What story of God was communicated to you? How was faith or spirituality modeled?

6. What were some explicit stories you were told growing up?

7. What were some implicit stories you were told growing up?

8. What disconcerting or painful memories do you find yourself reliving repeatedly even though you'd rather not?

9. What are a few things that you did either growing up or in your recent past that haunt you? That violate the person you want to be?

This is important work. Take your time recalling these stories and considering their impact. You'll need these answers as we move forward.

———

Now we make the transition to the final story—the culmination of the stories you were born into, the stories you were told, and the stories of the things you've done. All of these stories merge together with your personal experiences to form a unifying master narrative.

The master narrative is a story told over and over again in your own voice. This is the most powerful story in the world: the story you tell yourself.

CHAPTER 7

Stories We Tell Ourselves

This chapter is when everything we've talked about so far comes together. It's about reclaiming your power. About coming to terms with the most powerful person in your life:

You.

It's also about staring down and facing the only stories you can do anything about: the stories you tell yourself.

We've explored three different types of stories: the stories we were born into, the stories we were told, and the stories of the things we did. Some of our stories are similar to one another. Other stories are unique to us like a fingerprint.

As we discussed in the last chapter, these three types of stories build on one another and inspire each other. They all work together and impact one another, weaving together into a complex stream of stories. These stories become *the stories we tell ourselves.*

The stories we tell ourselves are the most powerful stories of all.

The stories we tell ourselves inform us of what we're capable of, what we're worth, what truth looks like, and where we can find answers. Our stories help us make sense of and move about the world. They run on constant loops in our heads—and go largely unchallenged and unnoticed. We just hear them all day. Always.

The voices talk and talk without stopping. They tell stories about ourselves and about others. We tell ourselves stories about people, places, and things. We repeat the stories to ourselves over and over. They become deeply embedded in our hearts, brains, and spirits.

From Theirs to Ours

It is critical to see how these stories transform from the story of a culture or a loved one to an embedded truth inside of you at the cellular level.

For instance, a story you were born into suggested that women should stay at home and raise kids. This became a story you tell yourself in the first person:

I have no options. My professional dreams are not important. My job is silence, avoidance, and peacekeeping.

Or, a story you were born into said that people like you don't go to college. This became a story you told yourself in the first person:

I am not smart. I'm destined to always work in this mill. I'm barely going to make ends meet like my dad and his dad before him. I will never know security.

Or, a story you were told suggested that you needed to lose weight to be worthy of a romantic relationship. This became the story you told yourself in the first person:

I'm too fat to be loved. I need to be loud and silly, or I must become invisible. I am ashamed of my body. I will reject love before love rejects me.

These stories become part of us. They are internalized and become our truths. Our realities. They become our distorted view of the world, through a glass darkly.

The stories we tell ourselves are nuclear weapons, live and active, resting in our chests.

When Our Stories Become Our Feelings

We don't make rational decisions when we're stressed or under attack. Our brain has default settings for fighting, running, or freezing to deal with heavy stress. When we tell ourselves stories, the reality of the stories—whether they are factually correct—doesn't factor in. Our stories become our feelings. Our body takes over.

In third grade I was in accelerated reading and math classes. I didn't try super hard academically, but I had enough natural gasoline in the engine to do well. Then a new opportunity popped up: I could test for WINGS[60]—the gifted and talented program at my elementary school.

My brilliant older sister was in WINGS, and some of my friends were in WINGS. Grades and academics were a big deal in my family—and I was confident taking the tests. The school saw my prowess. I got the invite. Testing for WINGS was the obvious next marker on my academic journey.

Except I didn't get in. I took the tests and I didn't qualify.

I concluded that I was not a smart kid. Which meant I was a dumb kid.

Talk about toxic shame.

Here were the facts: I was in accelerated classes, I made good grades, I read books, and I was intelligent. My parents loved me, they supported me, and I had excellent teachers guiding my elementary schooling.

---

60. I have no idea what the WINGS acronym stood for. Maybe Weird Introverted Nerds Growing Safely? Probably not . . . but maybe.

But as we know, facts don't matter under threat. I took this WINGS experience and the high value my family and teachers placed on grades—plus my environment, genetics, experiences, and relationships—and created new stories to repeat to myself. Stories like:

- I'm stupid.
- I'm not enough. I'm not any smarter or more gifted or more talented than anyone in my class and therefore I'm less than.
- My parents are for sure disappointed in me and probably ashamed of me.

Thirty years later, I have a stack of graduate degrees, three from a Research-1 university. I've spent my life running from the story that I'm not smart enough.

The story I told myself when I was nine is still hanging around. When I was working in universities, it would surface during tough academic debates. Or during research conferences. Or when I hung out with my brilliant mechanic friend Gustavo. Or my brilliant banking friend Todd. Or my brilliant heating and cooling friend Jon.

The story that I'm not smart enough or good enough shows up at the most ridiculous times.

And I know, I know—this is preposterous. Privileged nonsense. It's embarrassing to even be writing these things down. What a bratty, conceited, and unreasonable little nine-year old, right? And what a lame, insecure forty-plus-year-old.

But the truth is, thirty years later I have two PhDs, a certificate from Harvard, countless leadership and training certificates, and I've been a graduate school professor at multiple universities. I've won local, regional, and national teaching and service awards, been a bestselling author, and I co-host a popular radio-advice show and podcast.

And yet . . .

One of the default stories I *still* tell myself is that I'm not one of the smart kids. I still second (and third and fourth and fifth) guess myself. I'm still self-deprecating in the "hit yourself before someone else can hit you" kind of way. I still read brilliant science authors with a mix of jealousy, frustration, and awe, believing that I could never be one of them.

Remember how the stories stack up on one another?

The reason the story that I'm not smart is so painful is because it partners beautifully with another story I tell myself: I only have value if I'm smart. If I'm better than. So I spent nearly two decades chasing certificates, degrees, accolades, and trainings. Truth be told, I'd probably seek out more but my wife says that if I ever go back to graduate school for another degree (and any more nonsensical validation), I will be doing it as a single man.

And these are just a few of an endless stream of stories that I tell myself.

You have these stories too. Stories about how you're not enough. You're not good at things. Not pretty enough. Not safe or wealthy enough. That you're trapped. Stuck. Doomed.

These stories are powerful and heavy like concrete.

Hearing Our Own Voice

So how does this work? Why are the stories we tell ourselves so powerful?

The stories we tell ourselves are powerful because *we hear them in our own voice.*

This shift happens subtly, often over many years. The culture's voice or your abuser's voice or the coach's voice gently morphs into your voice.

An accusation begins as a knife and becomes a blanket. Dad leaves and you tell yourself that it was your fault. Or your girlfriend cheated on you and you wonder what's wrong with you. They called you ugly until you started calling yourself ugly.

There is incongruence because we beat ourselves up mercilessly—and we also think we're pretty good.

The stories we tell ourselves are powerful because we all think we're pretty smart. At least smarter than average. And we all think we're more honest than average.

Psychologist Dan Gilbert explains,

> If you are like most people, then like most people, you don't know you're like most people. The average person doesn't see herself as average. . . . Most students see themselves as more intelligent than the average student, most business managers see themselves as more competent than the average business manager, and most football players see themselves as having better "football sense" than their teammates. Ninety percent of motorists consider themselves to be safer-than-average drivers, and 94 percent of college professors consider themselves to be better-than-average teachers. Ironically, the bias toward seeing ourselves as better than average causes us to see ourselves as less biased than average too. As one research team concluded, "Most of us appear to believe that we are more athletic, intelligent, organized, ethical, logical, interesting, fair-minded, and healthy—not to mention more attractive—than the average person."[61]

So when we tell ourselves stories, we hear a voice we trust—our own. And our voice is smart and honest. Or at least smarter and

---

61. Daniel Gilbert, *Stumbling on Happiness*, (New York: Vintage Books, 2005), 252.

more honest than most people we know. And this way of looking at ourselves is powerful and compelling. When we have thoughts and feelings, we assume they're right. We *feel* like we're telling ourselves the truth. When we don't believe in ourselves or we don't think we're good at something, we believe we're right about those beliefs as well.

We craft tales and stories about ourselves and our surroundings that help us keep up the illusion of homeostasis or stability even when we're not safe, not doing what we want to be doing, or not accomplishing our goals. The stories we tell ourselves help preserve our illusions of control even as we sacrifice ourselves. We attach blame, causality, and power to these stories, and we repeat them over and over. We are the star and the villain of our own show.

And this is important, so don't miss it: *the stories we tell ourselves are often our way of making sense of someone else's issues by inserting ourselves as the main character.*

- I shouldn't have worn that dress.
- I shouldn't have asked her out.
- If I had cleaned up my room better, Dad wouldn't have left.
- I could never go back to school.
- I'm from a long line of non-sleepers. We just don't sleep.
- I'm not good at tests.
- I have [anxiety/depression/PTSD/ADHD/some other diagnosis] and that's why I can't do things that I want to do.
- I'm just not good at saving money.
- He cheated on me because I'm a lousy lover.
- I'm way too fat.
- I don't have a drinking problem.

Tragically, like the stories we're born into and the stories we're told by others, the more we tell ourselves stories, the more they become our default settings. They become what we say to ourselves without even thinking. Watch early *American Idol* episodes and witness Simon Cowell melt people with the truth about their lack of talent. I used to watch in disbelief as terrible singers would stand before industry professionals, singing their hearts out, believing they were good . . . when they clearly were not.

I can't tell you how many times I've talked with a young woman with an eating disorder or a young addict who didn't want to drink, but who also didn't want to hurt or remember either. The stories they told themselves were that they didn't look right. Or they'd always think about what happened. The stories they told themselves were stories of weakness, brokenness, and powerlessness.

We all do this.

And over time, we jump to these stories so quickly that we stop even recognizing that they're stories. We call them facts. We stop seeing them as the constricting nonsense they are and we blindly go about our days, silently repeating how great or horrible we are, what we should or shouldn't be doing, and then responding to the stories. We look for proof of them in the world, find the proof, and then start the cycle all over again.

And we wonder why we're burned out and exhausted.

The Three Types of Stories We Tell Ourselves

If we look across all the different types of stories that we tell ourselves, we can generally distill them into three distinct groups. The stories we tell ourselves are stories about:

- Ability
- Belonging
- Time

In the following section, we'll look at each one. As you read about them, notice which ones hit home for you.

Stories About Ability

We are born into stories about what women can do, what men can do, and what short people, tall people, skinny people, and over-weight people can do. We are born into stories of racial, economic, and geographical stereotypes. All these stereotypes are connected to different stories of abilities of both individuals and groups.

We're also told an incalculable number of stories about our own abilities—our abilities to love, to be "good," to make people happy, to achieve our goals, and to be loved in return. We tell ourselves stories about our intellectual ability, our physical abilities, and our work abilities.

Each and every one of us tells ourselves story after story about the things we can and cannot do.

My five-year-old daughter told herself she couldn't swim or jump off the diving board for years. Then, just the other day, she gathered up the guts to jump off the diving board. Now her story is one of courage. Where she told herself she didn't have the ability before, she now tells herself stories of ability. And strength . . . until it comes to riding a bike or climbing a tree or cleaning her room or punching the boy who tries to kiss her.[62] And then her stories of *in*ability rise to the surface again.

You and I do this same thing.

Again, these thoughts are generally automated, often going unchallenged in our minds. We either have data (i.e., I can't jump up

---

62. I can only hope.

and touch my kitchen ceiling, so I'm pretty sure I can't dunk a bas-ketball) or we are driven by our physiology or our feelings (i.e., that math problem looks hard, and I'm no good at math, so I don't think I can do this problem. And in fact, I can't figure out hard things).

Some common stories I hear about ability include:

- "I could never lose weight. All my family members are big."
- "I could never start a new business/degree program."
- "I'm just an addict. I can't stop drinking/eating sugar/work-ing too much/getting pissed off/spending money."
- "I'll never be able to pay off this debt."
- "They won't hire people like me. I'm stuck here."
- "Sex just becomes boring in marriage."
- "Women don't like sex. Men want it all the time."
- "Your body begins to ache as you age. There's nothing you can do about it."
- "I could never leave my cheating husband."
- "We can't just move."
- "I'll always be depressed and lonely."

My friend Justin McRoberts wrote an excellent book about his disdain for the phrase *It is what it is*.[63] This phrase, so carelessly uttered in our communities, is a statement of ability. A statement that says, "I am powerless." "I can't do anything to change this."

McRoberts wrote an entire book rejecting this sentiment . . . and I reject it as well.

When we tell ourselves stories, we often either sell ourselves short, convinced that we can't take action, can't achieve goals, or that we don't have control of big chunks of our lives . . . or we

---

63. Justin McRoberts, *It Is What You Make of It: Creating Something Great from What You've Been Given*, (Nashville: W Publishing, 2021), 4.

tell ourselves we have way more responsibility, control, ability, or capacity than we really do. We think we can keep our parents married, make some boy love us, or argue someone into changing their political or religious beliefs.

The reality, of course, is that you can't control whether someone likes you or not. Or if they think you're pretty. Or if they ultimately hire you. Or if you're a good fit. You can't control every single facet of your kid's life. Or whether your husband is an abusive jerk. You can't control that drunk driver who killed your friend. You can't control the cancer that took your mom way too soon. You can't control the hearts and minds of bigoted morons on social media.

But we spend devastating amounts of energy, time, and social capital on stories about how we *can* change minds, change hearts, or reunite cities or homes—when all we can really control or change is ourselves.

Remember, the stories we tell ourselves are about power.

They become stories about our abilities. About what we can or cannot do. And as Henry Ford once famously said, "Whether you think you can or think you can't . . . you're right."

Stories About Belonging

I remember the time I took my son to ju-jitsu class. I'd previously trained with the owner of the gym, and he invited Hank to join his special advanced youth class. We didn't have any kid-sized gear, so my son showed up wearing his little red shorts, a T-shirt, and socks. The rest of the class was wearing thick, professional, dark blue *gis*[64], and they were doing synchronized drills—more or less looking like

---

64. The name for ju-jitsu uniforms.

an army. Hank was skinny, not dressed right, and he didn't know any of the moves or drills.

After two or three minutes on the mats, it was clear to Hank that he didn't yet belong. He ran off the mats and I made him get back on. I told him he did belong. The instructor told him he did. The other students were welcoming and warm. But after one quick glance around the gym, Hank saw and felt enough to tell himself one of the most damning and crippling stories of all:

I don't belong here.

He jogged off the mat a second time, and out the front door of the gym.

I was disgusted with myself for not setting him up to succeed and then getting onto him for listening to his instincts. I should have never thrown my son into the advanced class without the proper gear. *Dad fail.*

In opposite fashion, I have friends like Jon and Jennifer and Tom and Patty in whose homes I know I belong. I can show up at their house, walk in the front door, and grab a drink out of the fridge. They have walked with me in some of the most formative, challenging, and blessed years of my life, and they've told me and shown me over and over again that I belong with them. That we're family.

The story I tell myself is that I belong with them and in their homes.

The feeling of not belonging activates our threat systems. When we don't belong, our body lets us know we're not safe. When we find ourselves out of step for a long period of time, the lack of belonging can set off the body's anxiety, depression, ADHD, and other connection-oriented alarm systems.

What about you? How often are you told you don't belong? How often do you tell yourself you don't belong?

That's what's happening when we don't go to the church event, or we don't apply for the job, or we don't pursue that girl, or we don't go to the concert. We skip the tryout, wear baggy clothes, or don't even comb our hair because we want to put out a vibe that says we don't care. We tell ourselves we're too cool to belong.

Or how often do we internalize the stories told by media, politicians, and community leaders who tell us we aren't welcome? What about those who have personally experienced the harrowing isolation of communities, states, or countries where they were explicitly told they didn't belong? How often do we look around and tell ourselves that we're not one of them (whoever *them* happens to be)?

But when we tell ourselves that we do belong, whether with our spouse, at church, with a political party, with friends from school, with a college sorority or a biker gang, our bodies co-regulate, and we feel safe and connected. Belonging is a core biological and psychological function.

Stories About Time

My mom did not go to college after high school. Like many women in the late '60s and early '70s, she was socialized to go to directly into the work force until she could secure a husband, have kids, and be a homemaker. During my childhood, my mom worked in the craft room at a local church and as a seamstress. It wasn't until she was in her early forties that she gathered up the strength and courage to buck so many of her internal stories and take her first community college class. The next semester she took another. And then another. And then another.

At age fifty-seven, she graduated with her PhD as a Medievalist. She became a tenured professor at age sixty-two and resigned from being department chair at age seventy-one.

My mom is a gangster who didn't listen to false or unrealistic stories about time, about age, or age-related abilities. One day she just decided to do what she wanted to do, when she wanted to do it. So many of us never make this decision.

The stories we tell ourselves about time often end up in two different camps: either *It's too late and I'm already out of time!* or *I have all the time in the world . . . so what's the rush?*

We tell ourselves we're too young. Too old. That it would take too long to get trained for that career we've always wanted. That the opportunity to reinvest, heal, and reimagine our marriage is gone. That "this is just what happens" as we age, at work, or in our community, or in our relationships.

My wife was hanging out one day with friends of hers—a husband and wife who were both thirty-five years old. Though the two of them were in medical-related professions, the couple disclosed that they really wished they'd gone "all the way" and studied medicine when they were younger. If they were to go now, they lamented, they each would be forty-two by the time they finally got out of med school.

This couple had concluded they were too late. They were out of time.

My wife sat quietly for a moment before speaking up. She finally said, "In seven years, you will both be forty-two years old. The real question isn't whether or not you're too old to start med school. The real question is this: In seven years when you turn forty-two, will you be doctors or not?"

Time is often an illusion. In my early forties I quit my career as a university professor and administrator to work on a radio show and to tour the country as a speaker. My wife transitioned from elementary school teacher to college professor. Then she quit her professor role to stay home with kids. Now in her early forties, she's a writer and running a successful coaching business for professional women.

At age forty-four, my dad left his job as a homicide detective to become a minister at a large church. In his fifties, he went back to being a police officer. At sixty-eight, he left the police force to become a university criminal justice professor. He has never been a professor before and this is the happiest I've ever known him to be.

I thought this was just how the world worked. I grew up thinking everyone did this.

I was wrong.

Most people get stuck. Get locked in. Get used to the same old thing.

This isn't just about work or career. This is about changing anything you want to change. Your character. Your relationships. Your faith journey. Your attitude. Your thoughts on a political issue. Your generosity. Being a better dad. Or a more connected brother. Or a bowhunter.

You're never too old to be a better husband. Or to say you're sorry. Or to lose those pounds. Or to try riding a bike. Or to go to a new church or to begin to understand God in a brand-new way.

Often stories about time start with the words, "I wish I would have . . ." or "I'll never . . ." I'll never be safe. I'll never be married. I'll never be free from this marriage. I'll never have enough money. I'll never have enough time. I'll never accomplish this dream. I'll never get rid of this weight that's dragging me down. I wish I would have made that call. I wish I would have apologized, or put my name in for that job, or kissed her back in college.

It's not too late.

Make no mistake: time is our most precious resource. Period.

We need to honor it.

Time is more precious than money, shiny toys, or winning certificates at work. When time is gone, it's gone. We can't get it back.

Time is often both a mythological barrier and a millstone around our necks. We almost always have more time than we think, while also never knowing when the other side of our ledger will be called. We simply don't know how much time we have. We are all an illness, car trip, or tragic incident away from being out of time.

You can't buy more time, manufacture more time, or circumvent time. With every minute we waste worrying or playing video games or complaining or saying, "I'll start that new degree program tomorrow," we cash out just a little bit more. We add another nail to our coffin.

Time is like spending from a bank account, and we don't know how much money is in it. It's best to be wise with our purchases.

It's almost never too late to start something new.[65] You're never too old to start over again. And you're never too young to get started. Wasting time on trivial or nonsensical things is a tragedy.

We often think too much time has passed us by or that we have all the time in the world.

Neither story is true.

The Power of Negative Stories

Like I mentioned before, stories can be both positive and negative. When stories are positive, they can open up new paths, inspire confidence, and provide expectation and accountability. They encourage

---

65. Of course, within reason. My dreams of playing in the NBA have long since sailed. I also haven't heard back on my application to become the second guitarist in the '90s glam metal band Poison. It's been like twenty years, but I'm ready if they ever decide to call.

us to shoot for the stars and land on the moon (or whatever that needlepoint sign in your guest bathroom says).

Positive stories are rocket fuel. Stories like: You can do hard things. You will smile again. You can rise above. Your mom and dad love you so, so much.

But if you're anything like me, your tendency isn't to reach into your history and pull out positive stories. As I mentioned in chapter 7, our brains don't want us messing around in the positive stories. We're programmed to watch for the negative ones. Our brains are filing systems for bad news, always scanning the world for negative stories. For situations that might hurt us, set us up to fail, or cause us shame or loss of life. Our brain also keeps a long record of the negative stories so that we don't get hurt more than once from the same thing.

Incredibly, when we spend time thinking about or rehearsing negative stories, we tend to see confirmation of them everywhere. As researcher and bestselling author Brené Brown says, "The truth about who we are lives in our hearts. . . . Stop looking for confirmation that we don't belong or that we're not enough."[66]

If we think that our feet are too big, we'll find ample evidence to confirm that theory. If we think people are always looking at our bald heads, we'll follow their darting eyes until they finally land on our most embarrassing feature. Someone told you that you have bad skin? You'll assume every wayward glance is looking at your acne scars. Not smart enough? You'll find a way to feel dumb every time you open your mouth.

Think your house has cracks in the ceiling and foundation? You'll see cracks everywhere you look.

---

66. Brené Brown, PhD, LMSW, *Braving the Wilderness: The Quest for True Belonging and the Courage to Stand Alone,* (New York: Random House, 2019), 158.

This is especially true of the stories we're told as children. Children absorb stories the way fire absorbs oxygen. Their hearts, minds, and bodies internalize stories as deep truths. These truths can alter gene expression, inflammatory responses, and learning abilities.

Negative stories put invisible limits on your life. They chain you to the floor—or to your old high school boyfriend or your old patterns of thinking. Negative stories create walls you can't see, ultimately trapping you. They tell you that you will always be the worst thing you've ever done. Or the dumbest thing you ever did. Or the meanest thing you ever texted.

I spent years not studying and just coasting through my courses because I honestly, secretly, believed I was dumb. Or I didn't want my stories to be confirmed. Studying would be a waste of time.

My little brother and my older sister had higher ACT scores than me.

See—I knew it.

I didn't get straight A's, and sometimes I really tried hard.

Told you so.

Proof was everywhere I looked.

But I can't outrun, out-earn, or out-achieve the stories I tell myself. You can't either.

We have to deal with them.

We have to turn and stare the old stories down.

All these negative stories once served a purpose. They kept us alive. Some of them kept us safe, or fed, or under a roof, even if we shared it with a dragon. But many, if not most, are no longer true. Or they're only half true. Or they're unexplored. Or they don't have to be true in the morning.

We pay a price for these stories. As Dr. Bessel van der Kolk notes, the body is keeping the score.

The Only Stories We Can Change

As I said at the start of this chapter, the stories we tell ourselves are about power. About our ability to change our lives in the course of a semester, or a weekend, or in an hour.

Or right now.

The bus wrecked with my students on it. I can't change that.

But I can write the story of what happens next.

You can't change your childhood abuse. It happened.

But you can own and determine the next chapter.

You can't change how your mom screamed at you, how your dad hit you, or how your wife left you in the ashes of a broken home. There is a period at the end of those sentences.

You can't change the story of what happened.

But you can change the story of what comes after.

You have that power.

In fact, it's the only power you have.

Your Stories

It's time to excavate the stories you tell yourself. Write down your answers to the following questions. Be as specific as possible.

1. Do you think you're smart? How do you know?
2. Do you think you're attractive or handsome?
3. Do you take care of your mind and body (exercise, relationships, nutrition, stress relief, reading books, journaling, budgeting, etc.)? Why or why not?
4. Do you take care of your relationships? How often do you talk and/or hang out with others? Why or why not?

5. What personal or systemic challenges or abuse have you experienced? Name them.
6. Who are your enemies? Who are the people intentionally seeking to make your life worse?
7. Who is in your corner, intentionally seeking to make your life better?

These questions are not the only ones to consider. As we go forward in the book, it's likely other stories will come to mind for you. Keep writing them down. The key here is to become aware of the stories you're telling yourself so you can deal with them for good.

In the next chapter, we'll discuss how our bodies spend all day working on our behalf to take care of us. Up until now, the idea of change has been centered around something we deserve. Or something we might want to do. In the next chapter, we'll see that change isn't just something for us to consider . . .

Change is something we have to do.

Let's start turning this ship around.

PART 2

The Stories Are the Solution

CHAPTER 8

Bricks in Your Backpack

"Will that be all for you today?"

The cashier was a kind, gray-haired woman. Through her exhaustion and boredom, she forced a smile in my dad's direction. She didn't seem to notice how nervous my dad was. He was a homicide detective and a SWAT hostage negotiator, so he was good at handling his emotions under pressure. But this was different.

"Yep, that's it," said Dad. He nervously looked around as the cashier scanned a small grocery basket worth of food. Milk, bread, beans, generic bologna, and some cheese. "Food for the kids," as he used to say.

Dad was nervous because there was no money in the bank account. Three kids and no money. And this was before the days of putting everything on a credit card. If there was no money in the account, there was no food.

His bank had just issued him a new item called a debit card—and sometimes it allowed him to purchase items that exceeded the amount he had in his account. This came with a massive overdraft fee, but it could get him out of a pinch. Other times, the card just declined the transaction altogether.

My dad was in an impossible situation: no money and no food. He worked a hard job and even had a few mowing and janitorial jobs on the side, but with three young kids, he often didn't have enough to make ends meet. Police officers didn't make much money, and sometimes he ran out of money before he ran out of month.

My dad was taking a calculated risk. He hoped the new debit card would accept the purchase and he could just pay the late fee on another day. His kids needed to eat today. Fingers crossed.

The gray-haired cashier looked up at my dad and said, "I'm sorry, sir, but the transaction was declined." My dad exhaled a heavy sigh of fatigue, frustration, and shame. He dug his thumb and index finger into his eyes like he always did when he was stressed. He started to say, "Thank you" and walk out of the store when someone called to him. Incredibly, the store manager happened to see this interaction from a few aisles over. She knew my dad. He had shown up in the middle of the night to help her and her family through a tough crisis.

She came over to the cash register and punched a few buttons on the computer. Without making a fuss, she bagged my dad's groceries, handed them to him, and told him he was good to go. She didn't charge him. She handed him the food and sent him on his way.

Let's look at this moment of kindness and grace through the lens of stories.

Three decades later, my dad still gets choked up telling the story of the woman who helped him feed his kids. The story where he worked really, really hard for his community and his family—and he still didn't have enough money for lunchmeat and cheese. The story where someone else had to step in and help. The story of loving his job as a detective but always wondering if he should go into business to make more money. The stories of his successful siblings, neighbors, and parents—and wanting to be seen as successful and enough. Stories of gratitude, grace, and unimaginable kindness. Stories of how a man is supposed to provide for his family.

These stories stacked onto his other, existing stories. Of the gnarly, gruesome things he saw at work. Of the bodies, the heartbreak, and the blood. Of talking people off of buildings and out of hostage situations. The stories of sitting with alleged murderers and hearing their stories and knowing deeply that but for a few circumstances, *he was that guy.*

My dad's stories were heavy, unwieldly, and always present. My dad's stories were bricks. And he carried these bricks with him everywhere. In some ways, he still does.

From this point forward, I want us to consider all our stories as bricks that we carry. From the stories we were born into and the stories we were told, to the stories of the things we did and the stories we tell ourselves.

My stories are bricks and your stories are bricks too.

And bricks are heavy.

The Bricks We Carry

We all carry stories. We all have bricks that we lug around in a backpack.

Some of us are born with few, if any, bricks to carry around. Maybe you were born into a community where everyone looked like you, laughed at your jokes, and took an interest in your well-being. The adults in your life valued you, held you to high expectations and high standards, and modeled the expectations and standards well. They walked alongside you when you fell short and they let you feel the consequences of your actions. Maybe you were tall, athletic, good-looking, or really talented in the classroom. Maybe your parents had a healthy marriage and they loved and connected with you deeply.

Some of us are born carrying a ton of bricks. Dad left you and your mom at the hospital. You were born into poverty, abused, or experienced physical or learning challenges. Maybe you didn't know the common language in your area. Maybe your mom wasn't well or your dad yelled about everything. Or your parents got divorced and you were convinced it was your fault.

Regardless of how many bricks you were born carrying, you also stumble across new ones over the course of your life. Some of these bricks you pick up and then toss on the ground. Others go into your backpack. Some bricks get removed from our packs.

Some stories aren't even bricks—they're pebbles that stay lodged in the cracks. Other stories are concrete cinderblocks. Mom abused you for years but told you that your dad would never forgive you if you said anything. Or your wife died in a tragic car wreck or your son took his life. Or maybe you took out six figures in student loans and you can't find work in your area. Or maybe you just got fired . . . again. Or your mom has Alzheimer's or you're on year three of IVF and you're still not pregnant.

Some of them were put there by culture. Some of them were put there by your family. Some of them were put there by your faith community, workplace, community, or government. And some of them were put there by you.

We don't want to think about them. We don't know what to think about them. Most often, we don't know they are there. We just get up the next day and then the next day, doing the best we can. And as the challenges and hurts keep coming, we throw them in with all the rest and keep moving. Keep living.

Just like the stories we tell ourselves—the bricks are our reality.

You are being crushed by the weight of these bricks.

Your body stays clenched. You don't take deep breaths. Your knees hurt, your hips are locked up, and your relationships are a mess.

If we are going to be well, we must be willing to stop.

Take the bag off our shoulders.

Set it down and unzip it.

And begin to go through it.

Each of us is responsible for taking the bricks out of our backpack.

For most of us, this is one of the most humbling, heartbreaking, and deconstructing actions we can ever take.

It is also the single bravest and most loving thing you can do for yourself. And for your children, your spouse, and your family legacy. Dealing with your bricks is a gift for your community, church, and even your country.

If you want to be well and whole, you must deal with the bricks in your backpack.

And this is hard because the vast majority of our bricks are trauma.

The Role of Trauma

We often think of trauma as the big car wreck, tsunami, heart attack—or when you find out your husband has been cheating on you after twenty-five years of marriage. As Bessel van der Kolk notes, "Trauma is an event that overwhelms the central nervous system."[67]

---

67. Bessel A. van der Kolk, M.D., Video: "When Is It Trauma? Bessel van der Kolk Explains," Psychotherapy Network, August 11, 2014, https://www.psychotherapynetworker.org/blog/details/311/video-when-is-it-trauma-bessel-van-der-kolk-explains.

But trauma is so much more than the single bad event.

Trauma is also neglect, not being seen, experiencing hard things alone, or any other experiential or environmental stressor that causes your body to take over and react for you, using its primitive response system. Trauma can be big or small, and it can accumulate over time.

This is super important: Trauma is cumulative.

So whether it's tiny pebbles, regular-sized bricks, or a single giant cinderblock, trauma is about the weight of your backpack over time. Big *T* traumas and little *T* traumas add up.

Taken all together, van der Kolk says, "Trauma is much more than a story about the past that explains why people are frightened, angry or out of control. Trauma is re-experienced **in the present**, not as a story, but as . . . bodily reactions, like a pounding heart, nausea, gut-wrenching sensations and . . . body movements that signify collapse, rigidity or rage."[68]

In other words, these stories aren't just in our thoughts. They are carried in our bodies. They're in our genes, in our blood, and in our hormones and neurochemistry. Until we deal with these traumatic bricks, and choose to set them down, our bodies will respond over and over again as though we are under attack in the present.

In the following section I will briefly explore how our bodies respond to the cascade of threats, ranging from things that happened when we were children to the present. Understanding how our bodies work, and how are bodies are trying to protect us, provides a safe step toward healing.

---

68. van der Kolk, *The Body Keeps the Score*, 206–207.

Our Ancient Operating System

I mentioned in chapter 3 that I really don't like technology or machine metaphors for discussing the human body. They can be helpful for context, but they often unintentionally box us in to seeing our minds, bodies, and relationships in ways that are not accurate—only representative. We often hear about our brains being "rewired" or new strategies being "downloaded." We hear of things like neural networks, or we tell our friends that our kid is having a "meltdown." Or how many times do we say things like, "I just need to let off some steam" or "turn off my thoughts"? Or that somebody's "brain is malfunctioning"?

Our bodies are not machines and our minds are not computers.

And while we generally know what we're talking about, over time these mechanistic metaphors can alter the way we understand how our bodies function. Think how different our responses might be if instead of saying, "Our kid is having a meltdown," we said, "Our kid is desperate to be seen and acknowledged." Or, "We've ignored our kid for weeks now, sticking him in front of a computer or tablet while we scrolled on our phones. Now his brain is registering the lack of parental connection as a lack of safety and he's lashing out with his limited communication tools in an attempt to reconnect."

But I digress.

Point is, people aren't machines to fix. They are not problems to solve. We need healing and relationships. Learning is not download-ing. Synapse growth and pruning new neural growth is not rewiring.

Even so, sometimes I find myself leaning on these metaphors too. In fact, I've already used them several times in this book.[69]

---

69. Alarms, operating systems, etc.

Reluctantly, I'm going to break my own rule again to make a point. The following computer analogy isn't perfect, but it helps me understand how trauma works in my body.

Our brains are running on an ancient operating system. Think your old Hotmail account or Windows 1.0. Yes, we've made civilian trips to space, created self-driving cars, and we have satellites in our yards that communicate to satellites in space. But our brains, hearts, lungs, and digestive systems are still very much the same as they have been for thousands of years. Our bodies are slow and predictable, and more than ever, they respond in ways that don't match our modern ethos.

As we've discussed, our bodies respond to a threat in four basic ways: running from it (flight), attacking it (fight), shutting down (freeze), and fawning.[70] There are a couple of other less common responses, but these three are the primary ones. Incredibly, our bodies respond to threats before we are even conscious of them. Our brain starts the fight, flight, or freeze response before we think about it.

For example:

- Maybe you've felt a premonition or a racing heart rate just as you turn into a dark alley.
- Maybe you slowly tensed up around the time your dad's car would normally pull into the driveway.
- Maybe you feel something is off with your spouse. You feel the gap between you but you don't know how to build a

---

70. Fawning is an attempt to please or gain favor with the threat. Raypole suggests that when fawning, "you escape harm . . . by learning to please the person threatening you and keep them happy." Crystal Raypole, "The Beginner's Guide to Trauma Responses," *Healthline*, August 26, 2021, https://www.healthline.com/health/mental-health/fight-flight-freeze-fawn.

bridge, so you grab another glass of wine, stay thirty minutes later at the office, or watch one more episode of some series.

- Maybe scrolling past certain news sites, feeling your work email notification buzz, or walking to check the mail cranks up your system without you even realizing it.

- Or maybe you were abused as a kid and your body still tenses up when someone comes up to hug you. Or your stomach hurts at night before bed or in the morning before school.

Whether you are consciously thinking of it or not, your body is keeping tabs on everything.[71] All the time. Like a vigilant watchdog. It's a security force that never sleeps, even when you're asleep.

This operating system worked brilliantly for the occasional lion or bear encounter back in the old days. When you had the misfortune of running into a threatening animal out in the wild, the body had a remarkable response-and-action system designed to keep you alive. But as Dr. Nadine Burke Harris points out, our bodies don't have a program for dealing with a lion or bear who lives in our home.[72] Or who rides the bus with us every day of our childhood. What are we supposed to do when that beast makes its way into our metaphorical backpack and haunts us when we're awake *and* when we're asleep?

The Basics of Trauma

As I said before, trauma can be "big *T*": like the car wreck, the death of a child, or the tornado that sweeps your home from its foundation.

---

71. van der Kolk, *The Body Keeps the Score*, 21.
72. Nadine Burke Harris, M.D., *The Deepest Well: Healing the Long-Term Effects of Childhood Trauma and Adversity*, (Boston: Mariner Books, 2018), 51–52.

It can also be "little *T*": the pebbles dropped into your backpack, day after day, year after year, weighing you down over time.

Secondary trauma[73] is what one experiences from working directly with those who are suffering or living difficult lives. Think of the trauma nurse, the EMS worker, the military veteran, the police officer, or the social worker. Think of the Title 1 elementary school teacher, the pastor, the lawyer, or the carpet cleaner who cleans up homicide scenes. Think of the dad with the special-needs child or the mom caring for her mother with dementia. You might not be directly impacted by the big *T* trauma, but gradually, just by your involvement in the lives of hurting or challenged people, you can pile up bricks in your backpack.

When my wife and I had six figures of student loan debt, a new house, and two nice cars, I noticed my heart would beat faster as I walked to the mailbox. In those moments, I didn't think back to when I was a kid and my dad went to the store to buy groceries knowing there was no money in the account. I rarely, if ever, think back to that time of tension and lack of security in my childhood. I don't make that connection consciously.

But my body makes that connection. It remembers everything. And so every time I made a trip to the mailbox to get my bills, my body geared up for a fight. Or to run. Or to shut down.

Every time my wife asks if we can talk about our budget. THREAT!

Every time I get the direct-deposit notice in my work email. THREAT!

Every time I see the stock market ticker or my wife says we need to slow it down on the spending for the rest of the month. THREAT! THREAT! THREAT!

---

73. Big-time shout out to my friend and mentor Dr. Lynn Jennings for her work on secondary traumatic stress.

My body remembers, and I respond to a question with a fight, or to a notice-to-pay by ignoring it, or to bad economic news by shutting down.

This is all trauma. An overwhelming and overloading of the circuits. A remembering in the deepest part of my brain and body.

Most of the bricks in our backpacks are trauma.

What Trauma Does

Pioneering trauma psychologist Dr. Peter Levine says that "people don't need a definition of trauma; we need an experiential sense of how it feels."[74] Harvard professor, trauma researcher and psychiatrist Dr. Judith Herman says that "in this state of hyperarousal...the traumatized person startles easily, reacts irritably to small provocations, and sleeps poorly."[75]

So again, don't think of trauma as the bad, horrible thing that happened in the past. Instead, think of trauma as your body's physical response in the present to what happened in the past. It's the physical manifestation of our negative stories. The constant spinning up of the fight, flight, or freeze response system, day in and day out, year over year, decade after decade.

It's trying to go to work, hug our kids, have sex with our spouses, go to the gym, and mow the yard while carrying a backpack full of bricks. (Almost impossible to do for very long.) It makes us just want to sit. Why do anything when it hurts to move?

Trauma disconnects us from other people and poisons relationships. How can we honor and take care of loved ones when our body

---

74. Peter A. Levine, *Waking the Tiger: Healing Trauma*, (Berkeley: North Atlantic Books, 1997), 24.

75. Judith Herman, M.D., *Trauma and Recovery: The Aftermath of Violence—From Domestic Abuse to Political Terror*, (New York: BasicBooks, 1997), 35.

is constantly at war with itself? How can we laugh, be sexy, or enjoy a night out with friends when our nervous system is on fire?

Trauma also disconnects us from our bodies. We react in ways that are out of character. We don't remember. Our bodies hurt. We don't sleep. We are distracted and unable to focus. I've heard stories of sexual abuse survivors who can recount the number of ceiling tiles in the bathroom where they were assaulted or who get nauseous every time they smell a certain aftershave, but who cannot remember faces or names of the men who hurt them. I've met with veterans whose heartbeats spin up at the sight of a speeding car or the sound of a slamming door. Their bodies remember even when they don't.

And as trauma disconnects us from our relationships and our bodies, it also disconnects us from our spirits. The bricks disconnect us from who we are. Dr. Herman says that trauma "destroys the positive value of the self, and the meaningful order of creation."[76] We stop living our lives oriented toward a better future and instead live in response to everything going on around us. We spend our days full of rage and anger, anticipating catastrophe. We cash in our needs to keep others happy. And all the while, we keep our heart a secret, cloaked in the guilt, regret, and shame that almost always accompanies trauma.

Disconnected from others, our bodies, and our spirits, we find ourselves unable to answer the two most basic personal questions: *What do I need?* and *What do I want?*

The cinder block plus the bricks plus the pebbles have left us immobilized.

We're too busy surviving and waiting for the next attack.

---

76. Herman, *Trauma and Recovery*, 51.

We're Not a Society of Weak Wimps

All this talk of stories and bricks and trauma can sound *woo-woo*. Like just another example of how we've all become a weak society, full of wimps and wusses. As if we're not as tough as we used to be.

This narrative is false. In fact, when I think of the bricks we're carrying just from the stories we were born into and the stories we were told, we may be the strongest generation in the history of the world. We are strong, strong, strong! But even the backs and knees of powerlifters wear out eventually.

Here is the truth of the physical toll.

When your body's fight/flight/freeze response system kicks up, it dumps cortisol and adrenaline and other response hormones, neurotransmitters, and neuromodulators, into your bloodstream. Every time your brain detects a threat or you try to lift that heavy backpack, the chemicals get spun up. Day in and day out, year over year, decade after decade.

It's like when you get a clogged sink. You can occasionally pour Drano down the drain to clear away the gunk causing a backup. But if you dump Drano down your sink every day, the chemicals will eventually eat through the pipes, destroy your plumbing system, and flood your house.

Dr. Nadine Burke Harris, a brilliant medical doctor, researcher, and current Surgeon General of California, discusses how ACEs— Adverse Childhood Experiences—have major and powerful medical consequences across a person's life span. ACEs include growing up in a house with divorce, toxic stress, parental addiction, or physical, sexual, or emotional abuse, among other types of environments.[77]

---

77. To take the brief ACES quiz for yourself, go here: https://developing child.harvard.edu/media-coverage/take-the-ace-quiz-and-learn-what-it-does-and -doesnt-mean/.

Adverse Childhood Experiences are the cinder blocks in your backpack. If you experienced multiple childhood traumas, or if you grew up in a home characterized by other people's drama and chaos, you are significantly more likely to have strokes, get cancer, have metabolic or heart disease, or suffer from major mental health challenges. The weight of the cinder blocks adds up and ultimately crashes your body. You will die younger.

Bricks in your backpack is not *woo-woo*. Your body can only take so much.

You Get to Choose

So here we are.

The stories are bricks. The bricks we carry around have a profound and lasting downstream effect on our bodies and our relationships. Many of these bricks are trauma, either the big cinder block or the tiny pebbles that accumulated over time.

All of us have experienced trauma. Whether or not you feel comfortable with that word, bad things have happened to you. Good things have *not* happened to you that *should have*. You have been hurt in real ways, and your body is still working relentlessly to protect you.

Remember, it's about the stories, the bricks you're carrying.

Heavy, destructive, and exhausting.

And . . .

You determine what happens next.

You can set the bricks down.

I would suggest that you have a *responsibility* to set the bricks down—to choose healing, forgiveness, wellness, and whole living.

You owe it to yourself. And you're worth it.

You owe it to your kids, your spouse, and your neighbors. They're worth it too.

We owe it to each other.

Yes, there are bricks you've been carrying for years—even decades—*and* you get to choose whether to keep carrying those bricks. You get to choose what to keep and what you let go of.

Most of us spend our entire lives trying to go back and edit the stories that have already taken place. We waste so much energy trying to change the past or ignoring the weight in our backpacks.

But the world is desperate for us to stop trying to edit the stories of what has been and begin writing and telling new stories. To write what happens next. What comes after the hurt and loss? What comes after you decide to own your stories and choose to be free?

What does life look like when you solve for freedom from the old stories and do the work to write new ones?

You get to make a choice right now.

This is Step 1 on the path to wellness: *Own your stories.*

The rest of this path is about taking action. It's about setting the bricks down, learning to write new stories, and choosing healing and wholeness over anxiety, debt, victimhood, and stagnation.

For some of you, this will require new levels of honesty, a change of daily practices, and a new commitment to honor yourself. For others, moving forward will require an overhaul of your life, including intensive therapy, medical care, changing your physical and financial health, getting a new job (or two or three), moving to a new city, or finally leaving your abusive relationships. It will require new boundaries and new ways of thinking. It may require you to learn new ways of talking to yourself and new ways to disagree with loved ones. It may require you to turn off the news, go back to church, tell your husband that you miss him dearly, or start spending time outside. You may have to lose a hundred pounds—or gain twenty-five. You may have to admit, "I was wrong, and I want to be better."

For most of you, this will be the hardest thing you've ever done.

Most people don't try.

You and your community are worth it, but you may not be ready yet. And that's okay.

You can't un-ring the bell of what you've heard thus far, but you can choose to ignore it. You can make excuses and say, "Delony doesn't know what he's talking about"; or "It's not the right season for me"; or "I have too much going on to do anything this drastic right now."

I won't be mad—it's your life. I'll still love you.

But if you're in, I'm in. Remember, there is a pathway to healing and wellness, and we're headed to Step 2 next.

CHAPTER 9

Acknowledge Reality: Good Grief

The past several chapters were difficult. Peering into your backpack to see all those bricks is tough. Unpacking your stories was hard, is hard, and will continue to be hard.

You had no idea how much weight you were carrying. How heavy your backpack is. If you're like most folks, you had no idea how often your body was spinning up into fight/flight/freeze in order to protect you from threats you weren't even thinking about.

You didn't realize you were hiding from your own life and how that hurts your kids.

You didn't know how far your life had spun out of control.

You thought anger and sore knees and the crick in your neck were normal.

You thought people just get bigger and grumpier and less mobile as they age.

You thought your food was healthy, that you didn't need to sleep, and your dad left because he was mad at you.

You didn't realize how your body was still replaying the trauma of your parents' divorce, all the yelling, or your deployment.

You thought you were mad at your husband when it was really your body remembering a time when you were unsafe.

You didn't realize your anxiety, depression, ADHD, your borderline personality disordor, or other diagnoses, were your body's responses to the bricks you were carrying.

You didn't know.

And now you do.

You've done a brave and hard thing. Most people never open the backpack and look inside. They never ask about the stories. They spend all their energy solving the next problem in front of them. And then the next and then the next.

They just keep carrying the old bricks and picking up new ones.

But you're done carrying the bricks. You're ready to set things down and break the generational curses.

Bestselling author Michael Singer says that "the reason you built the whole mental structure was to avoid pain. If you let it fall apart, you're going to feel the pain that you were avoiding when you built it. You must be willing to face this pain. If you were to lock yourself in a fortress because you were afraid to come out, you would have to face that fear if you ever wanted to experience a fuller existence. That fortress would not be protecting you; it would be imprisoning you."[78]

The only way to stop the cycle is to turn on the lights and come out of your prison fortress.

Begin taking the bricks out of your backpack and laying them on the floor.

After you own your stories, you have to *acknowledge reality*. This is Step 2.

---

78. Michael A. Singer, *The Untethered Soul: The Journey Beyond Yourself,* (Oakland: New Harbinger Publications, Inc., 2007), 135.

You have to stare down the space between what you hoped your life would look like and the reality of where you are. You started taking ownership when you began writing down your stories. Now you have to acknowledge where you are.

Acknowledging reality means you become radically honest about how far away you are from who you want to be. From the parent you want to be, from the financial position you want to be in, from the marriage and relationships you deserve, from the physical health you desire, and from the job that you want.

Acknowledging reality also means you become radically honest about the state of your relationships and the choices you've made. The truth about your childhood, your romantic partner, your kids. The truth about the childhood you didn't have and the opportunities that you were denied.

Acknowledgment hurts.

But it is the second step toward healing and wellness.

The Role of Grief

When most of us take an honest assessment of our past and present lives, we have to grieve. Grief is the gap between what you hoped or expected would happen and what actually did happen. The space between what you wanted versus what you received.

Grief is the pain and hollowness you experienced when your dad died. Grief is the inability to breathe when your brother went back to rehab, or the darkness you feel when you remember the guys in your unit who drove over an IED. Grief is the numbness you felt when your mom hit you . . . again. Grief is the blackout rage you felt when you stumbled onto your husband's secret email account. Grief is the denial that you're probably going to lose your job.

Grief is the sorrow you feel after the end of your marriage. Grief is experienced when you lose your wedding ring or you lose a child. You can grieve your wrecked 1988 Toyota Tercel hatchback or your dented brand-new Lexus. Grief is the grumpiness you experience when you sell the home you raised your children in and move to another one.

David Kessler says that grief is what happens on the inside; grieving or mourning is what happens on the outside.[79] Grieving or mourning is diving into the gap to experience the truth. To see and feel the truth with your own heart and mind.

You can be dragged into the gap by a great tragedy, or you can bravely head in on your own. But if you're going to heal, you have to spend time in the gap. You have to acknowledge reality and sit in it. You can't run from grief.

For many of us, we minimize or maximize our grief in comparison to others. We say things like, "Well, I know I lost my dad to Covid, but at least I had seventy good years with him. Janet lost her dad and he was only fifty." Or "I lost my job, but at least no one I love has died."

Or we say things like, "You think you're sad? You have no right to feel sad. You have all the money/cars/looks! *Look at what I'm dealing with!*"

Or we weaponize people's grief and bury them in shame: "You're the one who cheated. You lost your marriage and it's your fault. You don't get to feel bad."

Or we demand people shove their feelings down and away. We tell people to "get over it." That their feelings aren't real. We say

---

79. David Kessler, *Finding Meaning: The Sixth Stage of Grief*, (New York: Scribner, 2019), 153.

things like, "Suck it up. Cry me a river. Stop being melodramatic. You've got hungry mouths to feed."

You tell them, "I'll give you something to cry about."

Stop.

Stop comparing your grief to others. Stop judging other people's hurt. Stop trying to make yourself feel better by downplaying your pain or commenting on the pain of others. Stay out of their head and sit for a minute in your own heart.

Hear me clearly: *Never compare grief.* Ever. Comparing grief ends in resentment, destroyed relationships, and burned-down communities.

Kessler says that each person's grief is as unique as their fingerprints.[80]

Whether you are a person in power or a person on the margins; whether you are a millionaire or struggling at two minimum-wage jobs; whether you have committed great evil or your life is lived in service and dedication to loving others . . .

You have a right to your grief.

To your sadness. To your pain.

Every single one of us must mourn the gap between what we hoped for or expected and what happened. And it's disgusting, muddy, and dark in the gap. Grieving hurts and hurts and hurts.

However, it's here in the mud and the darkness that new growth begins. It is here that your body slowly feels and owns truth and the light breaks through.

It's where the imaginary cracks are seen for the illusions they are.

It's where we acknowledge reality.

---

80. Kessler, *Finding Meaning*, 29.

Big Grief and Little Grief

Some grief is little grief and experienced temporarily. You were hoping to eat at one restaurant and your husband chose another one; or you were hoping to walk your child into school for their first day of kindergarten, but Covid restrictions forced them to walk in alone. You hoped your wife would notice how many extra hours you've been working to help pay off your debt. But she didn't.

These losses are short-lived, but all are gaps between what you hoped for and what actually happened. Even the small, temporary losses must be acknowledged. Otherwise, they act like pebbles, weighing down your backpack.

Some grief—like the death of a child or spouse—can last a lifetime. This is big grief. Massive grief. Everything-is-different grief. This grief must be experienced over days and months and years. And it's not always physical death. Sometimes it is spiritual death or relational death or professional death. The loss of fidelity and trust, the loss of a church community, the loss of a job, or the loss of a good friend. You must walk through it, or at times sit in it—however grief works for you. Fighting it or running from it will keep your body on alert and inflamed forever.

Grieving is a practice. It's the movement toward the pain, where you take ownership of what has happened and allow it to integrate into your body. Grieving is allowing your amygdala to recognize that the threat has passed and allowing your frontal lobe to slowly come back online. It's acknowledging that the loss is real.

Grieving is about speaking the secrets in front of other people, shining light on the sadness or shame so that others can witness it, and living in the truth of your current experience.

Grief says your mom should have been there but she wasn't.

Your dad shouldn't have hit you but he did.

Your husband shouldn't have violated your marriage vows but he did.

That drunk driver never should have been driving but she was.

You thought you would get out of this town but you haven't.

You thought you'd be earning six figures and loving your job. But you're not and you don't.

You thought your new baby would make you happy and your marriage better. You love your baby but you miss the spontaneous, loving, fun person you used to be. And your marriage is still a mess.

I can't say this enough: Grief is acknowledging reality and feeling the difference in what you hoped for or expected and what actually happened.

Grief is ownership. Grief is truth.

What Grieving Looks Like

I have spent the past twenty years walking alongside others in their grief. I've done middle-of-the-night death notifications. I've held up mothers and fathers as they physically collapse to the ground upon learning their child has passed away. I've sat with friends who lost their marriages, and teens and adults who've lost their faith.

I have also spent time dealing with my own grief.

Maybe you have too.

We often view grief like we do our stories of death: we pretend it's optional. We think we can skip over the losses, run through them, or pretend they never existed.

You can't.

Grief is as much a part of our life as breathing. It's a part of our physical body and our spiritual body. Grief hurts, but it is not bad and it's not wrong. It's not abnormal. Grief is an exhale. A reckoning. Grief is the beginning of healing.

Grief is a gift.

Even if we don't consciously acknowledge what's happening, our bodies *feel* the loss. If we don't recognize and own the emptiness, our brain backfills the void with blame, sadness, bitterness, rage, resentment, addiction, and more. Our pain becomes a weapon, hurting us and those around us. I've said this multiple times throughout this book and I'll say it again: Our bodies will try to bridge the gap for years and years and years. Chemically, relationally, and through anxiety or depression or ADHD or gene expression or disease or chronic stress. Our bodies love us too much to let the gaps remain empty, and it will do whatever it can to step into the void.

Even if it kills us.

How to Grieve

There isn't enough space in this book to dig into all of the ins, outs, and practices involved with grieving. There are entire books written on how to grieve, and I've noted two of my favorites in the For Further Reading on page 263. That said, I do want to pass on a few things that have been helpful to me and those I've worked with over the years.

Grieving is a very personal yet communal experience. Everyone does it differently. So if you're new to peering into the gap, remember to be graceful and curious.

Sometimes grief is writing a letter to someone you lost. Grief is sobbing uncontrollably on your way to work. Grief is needing to go to the store but your body feels like it weighs a thousand pounds (remember the backpack) and you can't physically get out of the car. Grief is going for a walk with no destination in mind or timetable for return. Grief can be a black hole or on-to-the-next. Grief is feeling like you can't tread water for one more second. It's the undercurrent of rage that seeps out at the most inconvenient times.

Grief feels like falling and powerlessness.

There are good days and bad days. Sometimes minor incidents will roll off your shoulders or make you laugh, and other times you'll find yourself doubled over, crying so hard you can't breathe.

Acknowledging the loss always has value.

Here are some tips on grieving.

1. Grieving demands a witness.[81] For better or worse, grieving is social and external. *You cannot grieve alone.* And I know that when we're hurting, people give us stupid advice, quote pithy cliches, or they blame us or God or some political party.

   But grieving is about *not* keeping secrets. It's about being known and heard. About saying things out loud. We need other people when we're grieving.

   On a practical level, people bring us food, keep our kids, mow our lawn, keep us in check, clean our kitchens, and help us walk through funeral and estate paperwork.

2. Grieving demands clarity. I have found it incredibly helpful to write things down when I'm grieving. It's cathartic, clarifying, and powerful.

   It could be writing in a journal to yourself. It could be writing letters to the person you lost or the person who hurt you. It could be writing letters to your childhood self. It could be writing to your church, your friend group, your workplace, or others about how they can best honor and love you through this sacred, holy, ugly time.

---

81. Kessler, *Finding Meaning*, 29.

Pain increases as it gets more complex and more over-whelming. Writing things down gets our stories out of our head and bodies, and onto paper. It creates distance and perspective. Writing things down creates clarity.

3. Grieving involves honoring your body. Though it feels impossible to sleep, though you can't or don't want to eat, and though you just want the pain to stop, it's important that grieving be accompanied by exercise, eating, and sleep. These are often the last things anyone wants to do, but they are essential for keeping your body, mind, and spirit strong enough for the journey.

   You don't have to go to CrossFit or continue your marathon training. But walking or yoga can be transformative and healing. So is lifting weights, riding your bike, or going for a jog. Singing, dancing, cuddling, getting a massage—practices that involve touch and allow you to reconnect with your body—can also be life-giving. Eating as well as you can (who knows if all those casseroles are gluten-free, right?) and getting sleep are also critical foundations of your health. Keeping up a hobby, reading, going back to work, or finally writing your novel—these are all ways you can honor your physical and mental body.

4. When you're grieving heavy trauma or loss, it's important to remember that grief and grieving won't kill you—even when it feels like you're dying. Early on, grief can be like trying to survive the ocean currents. You're unable to stand up or to even get a full breath before the next wave comes crashing down on top of you. Your chest locks up, you're exhausted from kicking your legs and waving your arms, and you can't stop crying.

It feels like you're dying. You may even feel like you want to die.

Hang in there and keep treading water. Reach out to others. Over time, you'll find the water becomes more and more shallow and the waves have less and less power. You may find yourself swept up again by an out-of-the-blue tsunami even years later, but over time the ocean transforms from an endless body of water to a small creek. Or even a puddle. In the months or years that follow, you may notice that your feet are always wet but you're able to smile, laugh, find meaning, and even love again.

5. Disregard the temptation to "get back to normal." Grieving is the process of acknowledging something was lost and something new will have to grow up or be built in its place. One of the things we often do when faced with hard losses is to spend a ton of energy trying to get things back to the way they used to be.

The problem is, everything is *after* now. After the affair. After the new baby (and the next new baby). After Dad passed away. After you ignored the housework or after your boss told you to take the fall for the project delays. After you sold your old house and moved to your new one. After you got the job, but more money didn't make you happier.

After means there is no going back. Only moving forward.

Grieving is about acknowledging, owning, learning, and practicing remembrance that everything is different now.

Before we leave this chapter on grief, I want to provide a bit more clarity into our obsession with always trying to get back to the way things used to be.

When Things Don't Get Back to Normal

Without me even thinking about it, an imaginary mini-timer began running in my mind as soon as my wife and I got married. The imaginary clock was counting down the weeks, days, and hours until things would "be normal again." In my first job as a high school teacher and coach, I worked from before the sun came up until late into the night every night of the week, and all that time, I was eyeing this magical, mythical moment when life would go back to normal.

When my wife announced she was pregnant, my subconscious internal clock began ticking toward her delivery date. In my mind, once the baby was born, *then* we could return to our regularly scheduled program.

When we realized as a country that the Covid pandemic was going to extend beyond the "two weeks to flatten the curve,"[82] we all began looking for ways we could "get back to normal" in our schools, our businesses, our travel, and our relationships. We always want to get back to the way things used to be.

We say:

"He had an affair and I'm staying...I just want things to get back to normal."

Or "Our house was lost in a tornado . . . and I can't wait until everything is rebuilt so we can get back into our groove."[83]

Or "My husband died suddenly, and I know I have years of grief and recovery work to do. I just long for the day when I can feel like my old self again."

And so we wait for our past to catch back up with our present. Or we waste precious time trying to get our eighteen-year-old

---

82. Remember those days?
83. Let's be honest. Only Stella can really ever get her groove back.

bodies back, searching for the first-date excitement, or desperate for the feeling of innocence that came before knowing life can be torn away from you at any moment.

Here's the truth:

There is no going back.

The past is over.

The old days are gone.

She left you.

Your parents should have said they loved you and that you were beautiful, and talented, and smart, but they called you names and hit you.

The innocence is no more.

You cannot edit the sentences that have periods at the end. You can only write something new.

And as I said before:

The world is waiting on you to begin writing something new.

The best metaphor I've ever heard about rebuilding was used to describe the radical next steps needed to heal an ailing marriage that was reeling from infidelity.[84] The husband was deeply repentant, and the wife was committed to staying in the marriage. They both wanted to move past the affair, but they were using their past as the barometer for what moving forward would look like.

They kept trying to get back to their life before the affair, when things felt fun and spontaneous and they were twenty years younger.

They were chasing a ghost. That relationship was twenty years ago. And if they were honest, it wasn't so wonderful back then either.

---

84. I really wish I could cite this analogy because it is so, so good. If you know where you first heard it, please let me know!

Their therapist listened to them explain what they were looking for, and then said:

The citizens of New York could never gather up and recapture all the dust and shattered glass of the World Trade Center buildings. No number of electricians, welders, and tradespeople could untangle all the original materials (that were now twisted wire, steel, and concrete) to rebuild the Twin Towers.

The old towers could not be rebuilt with their old elements. The towers were gone. Lost in the ether. They remain only in photos and our memories.

The one path forward was to excavate the entire site. To clean out everything. Dig out all the broken stuff and even the stuff that looks salvageable.

It all had to go.

The citizens of New York had to hire an architect, an engineering firm, and several construction companies to design and build something new. Something stronger. Something that people hundreds of years from now will point to and say, "Wow!"

They had to set down the old bricks and write something new.

I think of this analogy almost every day.

As a culture, we should invite this type of thinking every time there are changes—big or small—in a marriage. In your life. In your job. A new kid. A major tragedy. A windfall of money. A broken leg. Mom goes into the hospital or the nursing home.

In big grief and little grief, this needs to be a regular rhythm of life: excavate, redesign, and rebuild. Create something new.

Your life will be different after the affair. After the third kid. After you get fired. After the divorce. After the 100-pound weight loss.

It will always be different.

But new doesn't have to be a cheap second.

It will be different, and you might always find yourself standing in water. You will never forget the past . . . and you wouldn't want to. It will always be there in your heart, in your children, and in your endless digital video library.

With careful planning, honest communication, and the right help and care around you, your *different* tomorrow can be meaningful and extraordinary.

And this brings us to the *how*. The *now what*. The actions needed to move forward.

I hope you're feeling a sense of empowerment slowly beginning to pulse through your veins. I hope you can see the tiny pinprick of light that just poked through the shroud. What comes next is about solving for freedom. Your freedom.

Freedom is scary too. It has a steep price.

It's about what comes next.

You've owned your stories. You've recognized the weight of the bricks you're carrying, and you have committed to yourself and your family that you're ready to set them down. For good. You've opened your backpack and begun to pull out the bricks, one at a time. You're writing down the stories and demanding evidence from them.

You've acknowledged reality and grieved the gap between what you wanted and dreamed of and hoped for and what your life actually looks like. You're committed to grieving. To sitting in the void, making peace with it, and then heading toward the light.

Whether you're reading this book in a laundromat behind your one-bedroom apartment or on a tropical beach in the Greek Isles, you're in the driver's seat now. We're going to turn our focus to the next moment. To our next brave (wobbly or strong) step.

There are no hacks, so don't look for them. No magic potions. No shortcuts. I'm not going to contribute to another shallow set of downloadable plans that make you feel good for a few days and then harden into yet another brick of shame and failure.

We're going to the root of true life-change. True wellness.

We're turning toward the future.[85]

Over the next three chapters, we're going to look at the other three key practices that will change your life. They're the infinity loop of peace: three principles, chosen over and over again. Three steps, taken over and over again.

Back in chapter 1, I told you the path was simple. It is. Super simple.

But I also told you it is incredibly challenging, especially in the beginning. Very few people live these principles. In fact, almost no one does.

But you've made it this far. You're changing everything. And the more you walk the path, the stronger you become.

Don't quit.

The last three principles on the path to healing and wholeness are:

- Get connected
- Change your thoughts
- Change your actions

That's it. So simple. So clear.

And so, so challenging.

Let's go.

---

85. "Where we're going, we don't need roads." Doc, *Back to the Future*.

CHAPTER 10

Get Connected

There were two couples sitting around my kitchen table: me and Sheila, and Byron and Jamillia. Our kids were playing somewhere down the hall. I waited until the laughter died down and there was a pause in the conversation. I was nervous.

"So this is gonna be awkward but I don't know another way do to it. I've got a question to ask you two, and you have to know this is gonna be weird, even for me."

When I announced I was about to be awkward and weird, the room got quiet. Very quiet.

I love people and am endlessly curious. I find most people wonderful and fascinating in their weirdness, uniqueness, and similarities. I love deep discussions, I love debates, and for me, very few conversational topics are off limits. So it shouldn't shock you that I have a reputation for asking personal—or as my wife calls them, "super inappropriate"—questions of both my friends and strangers.

"Well," Byron said. "Okay." He shifted a little in his chair and chuckled. I'm pretty sure he thought I was about to offer him a once-in-a-life-time opportunity to start selling Tupperware with me. He glanced at his wife. "This should be good. What's up?"

Now it was my turn to fidget. I caught myself looking down at my shoes, so I consciously looked him in the eyes, took a beat, and let my question fly.

"Sheila and I would like to know if you and Jamillia—*insert long, uncomfortable pause*—will y'all . . . ? We'd like to ask you two to officially be our friends."

Byron smiled like he was getting ready for a punchline.

But that was my question. It's all I had.

The air in the room got heavy. Sheila stifled a quiet cough.

Byron shook his head and said, "What do you mean 'officially be your friends'? We *are* your friends."

"Right" I said. "But we're letting you know that we will show up at 2:00 a.m. when you call. And if we need something at 3:00 a.m., we'll call you. We want our kids to know your kids and we want to celebrate your family . . . and we hope you'll celebrate ours. We are asking y'all to be our friends."

This was this worst. *What a stupid idea. Grown-ups don't ask other grown-ups to be their friends. I should have tried to get them to join a pyramid scheme.*

There was another long pause.

"Well, Delony, you're right," Byron said. "You just made this real weird."

Finding Friends

Let me back up a bit.

My wife and I had just moved to Nashville, and we were in the early stages of reimagining and rebuilding our marriage after a tough season. We were learning new jobs and a new city after living in the same part of the country for a couple of decades. We'd both spent our entire lives in Texas. Our families were in Texas. Our best friends were in Texas. Our professional connections were in Texas. We attended a tiny little farm church with people we loved. We had a tight-knit community and relationships we'd enjoyed for years. I loved my wife and she loved me, and we were both committed to our kids, but our ship had turned sideways in the harbor and we were stuck.

I was working my dream job in a wonderful city with wonderful colleagues.

And I was so, so lonely.

A few months in, it felt like the only people I spoke with outside of work were the other parents on my son's Little League team. Those conversations were hard to dig into.

"Hey man, how are you?" "Good, how are you?" "Good, glad to hear it." "All right."

"Wow, it's hot out today." "Sure is cool outside." "Think it'll rain today?"

"How's work?" "Work is good. How's work for you?" "Pretty good." "Okay, cool."

Repeat.

I knew the biology and psychology of loneliness. I knew the science said my body is a connection-seeking machine, always scanning the environment for who's in my tribe, who's walking through life with me, and where I might be socially or physically out of step.[86] I knew the key to all physical, spiritual, relational, and mental health is belonging. I knew being lonely was physically more damaging than smoking fifteen cigarettes a day.[87]

---

86. Review chapter 3 for a refresher on loneliness.

87. Julianne Holt-Lunstad, Timothy B. Smith, J. Bradley Layton, Social Relationships and Mortality Risk: A Meta-analytic Review, *PLoS Medicine*, July 27, 2010, https://journals.plos.org/plosmedicine/article?id=10.1371/journal.pmed.1000316.

I also remembered how my last few experiences with loneliness ended with me crawling around in the dirt or trying to slink away from my work, church, and family relationships. I understood how living life without friendship, love, and connection was choosing a slow, suffocating death.

I knew I needed other people on my team, and I knew I had to be intentional and drastic.

Also, it wasn't just about me. Sheila and I both understood that we needed people we trusted to walk with us as we figured out who we were going to be in this new chapter of our life. We knew we couldn't heal our marriage and create something new and extraordinary without others walking alongside us. We needed friends to know and love our kids, and we needed other kids to know and love us. My wife and I couldn't live life in our new community alone.

I knew all of this in my head. I felt it in my heart.

I just had to do something about it. I had to act.

So, Sheila and I started inviting people over to our house. We started saying yes to every invitation. We met with people from our past who lived in Nashville. Folks from our new church. Folks from our block. Our goal was to connect, love, and risk. The "this just got really weird" couple are still close friends. They laughed off my weirdness and we still see them regularly.

The second couple we invited over was Aaron and his wife, Erica. Same deal. Same house. Same chairs. Same painfully awkward question. "Will you be our friends?" Same weird pauses and same heavy, thick air.

Only this time something different happened.

Aaron sat quiet for a moment and then glanced at his wife. Without warning, a tear began rolling down his cheek. The silence remained for a moment, and finally he spoke up.

"Nobody's ever asked me that before."

Erica put her hand on his shoulder. The conversation went in new, unexpected directions and we talked for a long time.

Sheila and I had new friends.

You Cannot Be Well Alone

The third step on the path to healing and wellness is to get connected to other people.

You cannot do life alone. And though we've already talked about this in previous chapters, let me reiterate how important human connection is.

I do not believe you can ever truly know who you are, what your purpose is, or what you truly believe, outside of your relationships with others. We are who we are because of our relationships.

We are designed for connection—to live in tribes, teams, communities, units, gangs, whatever you want to call it. When we are alone, our bodies sound the DANGER alarms over and over and over. The alarms of anxiety, depression, mental illnesses. The alarms of physical pain, chaos, and addiction.

We are social creatures—our physical bodies need to be in the presence of other physical bodies. Humans are co-regulated, meaning that our biology, physiology, and psychology are regulated in connection and relationship with other people. In the absence of nurturing relationships, babies die, children become dysregulated, and adults implode.

This is about physiology, psychology, and spirituality. It's as complex as brain chemistry, hormone function, and gene expression. It's also as simple as someone bringing you tacos when you're grieving or helping you change a tire in your driveway.

You cannot be well by yourself. You must have other people in your life, walking alongside you, doing life with you. Period.

Put another way, other people are your emergency fund for life. It's not a matter of *if* bad things will fall in your lap—it's a matter of *when*. Moms get sick. Dads have heart attacks. Enemies attack. Spouses suddenly pass away. Girlfriends cheat, companies downsize, economies crash, and kids make terrible choices.

If you want to find wellness and peace, you have to be connected with other people. Same as me. Same as everyone.

A Horrific Paradox

And yes, I see you sitting on your hands in the back, introverts. Yes, I see you "I've lived this long without people" people. And yes, I can be an "Other people stress me out and I'd rather just do this alone" person.

I see you all. I am some of you. And the hurt is real.

When you've been without people for a long time, or when your greatest comfort is in solitude, connection can be hard.

If you've been abused or experienced relational trauma or neglect, connection with other people can feel overwhelming and destructive. It can feel like you're in a performance, trying to force a smile while also not falling off the stage. Every time you get close to someone, your alarms sound, your body identifies a threat, and you bail. Your heart races. Your hands clam up and your throat clenches. You feel like you're drowning in your own body. You just want to crawl under the covers. You want another drink. Or you want to hook up but not get close.

One of the reasons sexual, verbal, and physical abuse is so traumatizing and evil is because abuse weaponizes relationships. Abuse turns relationships into poison.

It's like being lost at sea and dying of thirst, but surrounded by the wrong kind of water.

Trauma and abuse send signals to your brain that other people are dangerous and can't be trusted. Parts of your brain identify trusting relationships as *not safe*. At the same time, you and I need trusting relationships to breathe. We need connection to survive.

A paralyzing dilemma.

Especially because I know you've been hurt. Me too. I know the people who were supposed to love and care for you didn't. Or they did love and care for you, but they did it in a clumsy way. They said things the wrong way. They had the wrong reactions. They stole from you. They left you.

Through their actions and words, they told you stories about your lack of worth and your lack of value. They became bricks in your backpack.

Or maybe you've been married for forty years, have several kids with your spouse, and your spouse has no idea who you really are. He or she doesn't know you. Or you work in the same office year after year and your colleagues never fully understand you. The risk is too great. The cost of getting hurt again is too high.

Maybe the detachment and loneliness have kept you safe. They served a purpose for a season. Or maybe even for your life so far.

But you're here because you want more for your life. You want to be well. You want to heal.

So you have to reconnect.

With family, extended family and in-laws, neighbors, church members, work colleagues, or friends.

Whoever and whenever. Whatever works for you, in whatever order you need.

No more excuses. No more defenses. No more masks.

It's time to set the bricks down. To find connection. To be vulnerable and risk again. If you're serious about being well and having peace, you have to get connected. You must have people you can count on. People you can serve and show up for. People who will serve and show up for you.

It's the only way.

This Is Hard. Do It Anyway.

Look, I know. I'm not an idiot. This sounds stupid, childish, and like something you're not going to do. Maybe you're a stay-at-home mom with three kids under the age of five, or a long-haul trucker who only sees other people at drop-offs and while grabbing a quick shower at the truck stop. Maybe your family hurt you, your work environment sucks, and the idea of making friends is absurd. I get it.

Trying to heal old family relationships—or even just be honest with family—is hard. Trying to make friends in a world built around independence, tall fences, and No Trespassing signs is difficult. Trying to create deep, meaningful community in a victim-oriented cancel culture can be grueling.

Dr. Gabor Mate says,

> We sometimes find it easier to feel bitterness or rage than to allow ourselves to experience that aching desire for contact.... Behind all our anger lies a deeply frustrated need for truly intimate contact. Healing both requires and implies regaining the vulnerability that made us shut down emotionally in the first place.... We can permit ourselves to honor the universally reciprocal human need for connection and to challenge the ingrained belief that unconsciously burdens

so many people with chronic illness: that we are not lovable. *Seeking connection is a necessity for healing.*[88]

Look around at our world and you'll see how true Dr. Mate's words are. It is easier to be angry all the time. It is easier to let our fight/flight/freeze system live our lives for us. It is easier than trying to make friends. Trying to reconnect with family. Trying to let messy people into your messy life.

But you have to.

It feels impossible, but it's not.

All relationship is risk. Every single one. Risk that you might get rejected (again). Risk that someone might break your heart (again). Risk that you might get burned (again). Making friends, especially as an adult, will always be hard and awkward for most people.

Do it anyway.

And I want to be clear: This is not all "out there" in the world. Some of us need to reconnect inside our own homes. With our spouses. Millions of people share a bed with someone they barely know. Or share homes with children they don't know—or even like. We're clear on how our spouses take their coffee, but we don't have a clue about what spiritual issues they're wrestling with, what their dreams are, or why they've settled for a C+ life. Quite possibly the same can be said for our kids.

Our bodies and souls are screaming for connection. Remember the loneliness epidemic? For most people, relationships conjure up fear.

But it's not just about fear. It's also about practicality. There's just not enough time. When you're working a full-time job (and a

---

88. Gabor Maté, M.D., *When the Body Says No: The Cost of Hidden Stress,* (Hoboken: John Wiley & Sons, Inc, 2003), 279.

side job or two), going to the gym, trying to squeeze in some graduate school, and dealing with your spouse and your kids, it can be
hard to get to bed on time, much less develop new friendships. Or
deal with family drama. Or pretend to be friends at work.

And it's more than this. It's also about the complicated dynamics
involved with family[89] and work. You know the drill. You have in-laws.
Your parents. Your cousins and aunts or uncles and all the support,
opinions, confusion, anger, love, and neglect that come with those
relationships. And the workplace connections. Your friends and
bosses and teams. The networking, mentoring, demotions, and promotions. The hiring, firing, and taking livelihoods away. Some family
and work relationships are super close; some aren't safe. Some work
relationships are invaluable, and others are abusive.

Point is this: you must choose and you must connect.

Friendship

There are a lot of relationships you don't get to choose—family, your
in-laws, your work colleagues. You usually don't get to choose your
neighbors or your kid's teacher either.

A million books or more have been written on family dynamics
and work relationships, but there's not a lot out there on the art of
friendship.

Of course, work colleagues can become our best friends—but
those relationships can be laced with deep challenges. Our adult
family members[90] can become our friends, but those are also

---

89. I'm giving family its own category.

90. You cannot ever, at any time, for any reason, be friends with your young
children. Not until they're at least out of college (at a minimum). You can be very
close and love being in relationship with your kids. But they are not your friends.

lined with relational land mines. Neighbors can become your best friends in the world, or they can play pop-country music into the wee hours of the morning and peel out their tires for no reason.

All told, the story of friendship covers a lot of territory.

So for the rest of this chapter, I want to take a deep dive into friendship. What it is, what it's not, how it works, and how to be good at it.

And yes, this sounds ridiculous—like we're back in kindergarten.

Get over it. We have to start where we are.

And even if you think you've already got all the friends you'll ever need, keep reading. Friends move. Friends fall out. Friends grow, change, or start talking about CrossFit all the time. You could probably learn to be a better friend. I know I can.

So we're starting back at square one. At how to connect and make friends, and how to become a better friend, partner, and citizen.

Don't skip this section. You need it. We all do. This is how you survive and thrive during an epidemic of loneliness.

As we dig into connection, I want to first paint a picture of what friendship really is.

What Is a Friend?

Let's take it from the top: What is a friend?

We talk to each other with words, but we typically think in pictures. We throw the words *friend* and *friendship* around all the time, but we all have different views of what they mean.

Let's start with what a friend is *not*.

They cannot handle the weight of your adult world, and it is unfair to involve them in a one-way, power-laden friendship. Get your own friends and let them have their own. You just stay Mom or Dad.

Remember, a friend is not a click or profile pic. A friend is not someone to text with now and then or hop online with for an hour of *Call of Duty* (unless this is part of a longer, deeper, established connection). A friend is not someone who only double-taps the heart emoji when you post pictures of your cat.

Connected friendships exist separate from screens and digital mediums.

A friend is also not just someone you see regularly at work. Someone you chat with or vent to or join at a local bar after hours to blow off steam. A work buddy or a work wife.

Is your neighbor a friend because you live next to him? Is the woman at the park a friend because your kids play together several times a week? Is that person you see at church your friend because they sit close to you?

Friends aren't based solely in the past. Those old high school or military buddies or college pals you had years ago? They're not your friends if you haven't talked to them in years.

Friends aren't disposable. If you cut people out of your life when things get tough or weird, your relationships are the equivalent of those single-use cameras we all bought for prom back in the '90s. Friends screw up, make mistakes, and ask for forgiveness. Friends accept apologies and forgive. Friends say "I'm sorry" and go forward together.

Friends aren't selfish. Friendships are not about "return on investment" (ROI). Real friends are about mutual connection and support, not about advancing your position or trying to get things from each other.

Friends don't perform for one another. Friends accept you for all your glorious weirdness and brokenness—and love you anyway. If you have to impress your friends or constantly be "on" in front of them, it's not friendship. It's a performance. Real friendship means you can be yourself.

Friends aren't shallow. They're not your spouse's friends or the people you nod to on the street. They are people you know, invest in, and care for. They are people you challenge, hold accountable, argue with—because they're worth engaging with.

Friendship isn't caretaking or codependency. The people in your life who drain you and constantly ask for more are not your friends. A friend is not someone you need to fix or help so you can have esteem. Friendship means giving *and* receiving.

Being a friend is both something you do and an identity—something you are. And importantly, friendship is a skill. It's something you can learn. Something you can practice and get better at doing.

You can improve at identifying possible friends, opening up and being vulnerable in your friendships, benefiting from those relationships, and even knowing when it's time to let a friendship flame out.

And let's be honest about this: friendships feel like they shouldn't be so hard—like if they were meant to be, they should just happen. But renowned psychologist and bestselling author Mihaly Csikszentmihalyi offers a different perspective:

> People believe that friendships happen naturally, and if they fail, there is nothing to be done about it but feel sorry for oneself. In adolescence, when so many interests are shared with others and one has great stretches of free time to invest in a relationship, making friends might feel like a spontaneous process. But later in life, friendships rarely happen by chance: one must cultivate them as assiduously as one must cultivate a job or a family.[91]

---

91. Csikszentmihalyi, *Flow*, 189–190.

When we're kids, for better or worse, adults dump us onto a recess field or in a room and say, "Go have fun." You do assignments together. You get stuck around lunch tables or in youth group vans together. You throw rubber balls at each other and play with the giant parachute.

Now that we're adults, we sit next to each other in matching minivans in the carpool line and it feels like we're on different planets.

A Question of Friends

Here's a picture of what friendship looks like to me. It's 3 a.m. and your spouse gets sick. Really sick. Like, it's time to go to the hospital and get this figured out sick. One problem: your kids. You need someone to come keep an eye on them while the two of you see a doctor. Your parents live in another state. Same for your in-laws. No babysitter is answering the phone at 3:00 a.m.

Who do you call?

A friend. Someone you can trust in the middle of the night to watch your kids, sleep on your couch, and get them to school. Someone who cares about you enough to not just answer your call but to hop in the car. "I'll be there in fifteen. It's gonna be okay."

Or, you just lost your job. You said something that really hurt your wife. You hit your kid. You're happy looking at your newborn baby but crushed that you've lost your old freedom.

Who do you call?

Friends.

Here are four questions you can ask to evaluate whether the people in your life are just acquaintances or actual, genuine, real-life friends.

Question #1: Can You Tell Them the Good Things?

Our culture doesn't encourage us to celebrate one another. Tony Robbins says we're a culture addicted to problems, and we lead butt first. We don't greet each other with the best things going on in our lives—we hide them—and greet each other instead with the dire news or the pessimistic stock market predictions. We are a culture of whiners and complainers.

This is a stupid and absurd way to live.

Real friends are the people you like to call when you have good news. Why? Because they are genuinely excited for you. They celebrate you. They cheer you on. They are genuinely happy to hear what you've got to say.

- "I got the promotion!"
- "My article got accepted."
- "Dude, she said yes!"
- "I shot a 2-under."[92]
- "It's a girl!"

Big moments we instinctively share with others, right? We post them. Text them. Broadcast them. Sometimes we run down the sidewalk shouting at anyone who will listen. It's easy to share that kind of good news.

But what about the little details of your day? What about the stuff that brings you joy? Who do you tell that stuff to? The boss told you, "Good job." You had a killer workout or saw a hilarious meme.

---

92. I have a whole other problem with being friends with golfers . . . but that's for another book. Carry on for now.

You crushed a presentation at work and just wanted to share that with someone.

- "We're finally having sex again."
- "I used to hate this politician but he changed my mind on this policy."
- "I'm trying to be a grill guy and you know how I usually suck at it? Well, I finally nailed it last night."

Let's be honest: Some people have no interest in hearing that kind of news. Some people have no interest in those kinds of conversations. Maybe they find them boring. Or beneath them. Or they just don't care about you enough to understand why you think this is a topic worth discussing.

Those people are not your friends. Not the kind of friends you can count on.

Friends are people you can share the good things in your life with, big and small.

Question #2: Can You Tell Them the Bad Things?

As I mentioned, we have a culture built on whining, complaining, leading with bad news, and tearing down. We've turned the good life into a sum-zero contest. Our conversations are filled with complaints about who screwed you over, who made your life harder than it needed to be, who slept with who, and who's making more money than you. But that is usually surface-level whining.

Complaint-driven drivel is not what I'm talking about.

I'm talking about when you've messed up. Who do you call when you make a mistake or do something that violates your core values? Do you have people who will be pissed, hold you accountable, and let you have it?

Friends who will scream at you, take a swing at you, and then bail you out and go to court with you?[93]

Because that's what friends do.

Who can you call when you absolutely blow it?

- "I can't believe I called her back. I promised I wouldn't do that again."
- "Three months without a drink, but I just lost it, man. I need you to come get me."
- "I'm about to be an empty nester and I don't have anything to do next."
- "I should have done my homework on the merger. Now I'm probably out of a job."
- "I slapped my kid. I'd had a third glass of wine and I just slapped him. What is wrong with me?"

There are lots of people who would like to hear the juicy details of your biggest flops. But can you trust them? Is it safe to talk with them? Or are they relational vampires who feed off you and then whisper behind your back? Because those people aren't your friends.

A friend is someone you can be deeply honest with.

Question #3: Can You Tell Them About the Darkness?

Take a look back at the stories you've written down. The bricks in your backpack.

Is there anyone in your life you could talk to about those memories? What really happened? If your parents, or sister, or brother come to mind, count yourself blessed. Except in rare cases, I'm not talking about your family.

---

93. Everybody, relax. I'm not saying your friends should hit you or beat you up ... it's just a metaphor.

Do you have friends you can talk to about your trauma? About the times you were hurt? Who can sit with you while you unpack your bricks and practice setting them down for good?

Similarly, these are people you can call out when they hurt you. You can tell them you don't like something they said or did.

- "The other day when you made that joke about my weight—I know you were kidding, but I didn't like that."
- "My dad left us when I was a kid."
- "I was molested as a middle schooler."
- "I've got to draw the line at those words. Don't say that around me."
- "Your son is getting a little too aggressive with my daughter."
- "That's not funny . . . even for me. Be better than that."
- "I saw that movie you recommended and it was awful."[94]

A true friend is someone you can tell about your deep hurts and they will listen, not load you up with dumb advice or cliches. Then they'll come back the next day and let you talk some more.

Question #4: Will They Show Up?

Finally, you will know a true friend when they show up. Like I mentioned earlier, who can you call in the middle of the night in an emergency? Who will drop you off at the airport for the early flight, go with you to get a tattoo, or worst of all, help you move?[95]

---

94. I used to recommend my favorite movies and punk records all the time. My closest friends came to think of me as a lunatic. They told me that me and my movie choices were terrible.

95. Moving. Is. The. Worst. Only the best people show up to help others move. If you've ever helped someone move, you are legit. Thanks for being a good human.

Who would show up? Who values you enough to put their money where their mouth is?

I'm not just talking about the big stuff. If your kid was in her first game as a starting pitcher on the varsity squad, would your friends come to watch? Would they even know about it? Who can you call right now and say, "Hey, I'm reading this crazy book by some guy with a radio show, and I need to unpack what he's saying. Can we grab lunch tomorrow?"

Real friends show up for each other on a two-way street. I've got your back and you've got mine. That's the kind of connection you need if you want to change your life.

I once received a call from Todd, one of my dearest friends in the world (the same friend who drove three hours to see if my house was falling down). I met him in my freshman dorm and we've been friends ever since. Todd is my most stable friend. I'm pretty chaotic, and he is even keel. He's responsible, a banker, and he understands things like federal monetary policy. He tucks his shirt in and only drives Fords. He's had the same haircut for over forty years. He's that guy—and I love him for it.

We talk a lot, so the phone call itself wasn't a surprise. But what he said shocked me.

Todd: "Dude, my bank just got sold."

Me: "Oh yeah? So are you rich or what?"

Todd: "Man, I think I just lost my job."

If I could have picked which of my friends was the *least likely* to lose their job, it would have been Todd. No one else would have even been close.

Me: "Whhhaaattt? You can't get fired. You're my only stable friend!"

We laughed a little, and he walked me through the bank sale and then what he might end up doing next. We talked about his financial situation, his family, and how his wife (another one of my close friends) was doing. Then, later in the call, I piped up: "Well, speaking of getting fired, I just found out I made the bestseller list."

Todd: "*The* bestseller list? For your little Anxiety pamphlet book?"

Me: "I know, right? I didn't see that coming. I'm pretty freaked out that people are actually buying this thing."

Todd: "You should be. That doesn't make sense at all. But if that many people bought it, good for them." We both enjoyed the laughter and the inside jokes.

Then he said, "Dude, that's great news. You've been working so hard on all of this for so long. That's really great."

In one phone call Todd and I shared the good and the bad. We told the truth, both up and down; we talked about fears and what was to come next.

That's friendship.

Bad times will come for all of us. Good times will come for all of us as well. As the great line goes, we don't need to be fixed . . . we need a witness.

Friends are our witnesses to the good stuff, the bad stuff, and the dark stuff. Friends show up. They bail water. They fix shingles. They mow lawns and they sit on your couch and say, "We love you too much to let this continue." We were made to run in packs or tribes.

When you are connected with true friends, you are better equipped to handle whatever the world throws at you.

Take an Inventory

If you're going to be intentional about getting connected, you have to figure out whether—and to what degree—you are already connected. So let's take a quick relational inventory.

Do you have friends who line up with the picture I just described? Do you have people in your life who you tell the good stuff, the bad stuff, who listen when you talk about deep hurts, and who show up when you need them?

If so, write down their names.

Most people in Western culture are starved for true friendship. Some research shows up to 75 percent of people don't have *anyone* they could call for help in the middle of a crisis.[96] It's why we have hotlines.

If you've got one real friend, you are blessed. If you have two or three or five, you are rich beyond measure. You are in rare, rare air.

If you've written down a few names, call those people today and tell them how grateful you are to know them and enjoy their friendship. Take them out for coffee. Buy them a burger and a drink. Write them a letter. If you don't know what to say, say something anyway. Don't let them go any longer without letting them know what a difference they make in your life.

If you don't have any names written down on this page—if your relational inventory is empty, or if it's filled with "if" and "maybe"—you know you've got work to do.

Remember: All relationships are a risk. Fortunately, friendship is a skill—it's something you can practice and improve. You can grow personally as a friend, and you can grow the number of friendships in your life.

---

96. Ellen E. Lee et al, "High prevalence and adverse health effects of loneliness in community-dwelling adults across the lifespan: role of wisdom as a protective factor," *Cambridge University Press,* December 18, 2018, https://www.cambridge.org/core/journals/international-psychogeriatrics/article/abs/high-prevalence-and-adverse-health-effects-of-loneliness-in-communitydwelling-adults-across-the-lifespan-role-of-wisdom-as-a-protective-factor/FCD17944714DF3C110756436DC05BDE9#.

How to Make Connections

So how do we actually make friends? Real friends? Here are six ways to begin.

1. Make it a priority and decide you're going to do it.

Accomplishing anything starts with a goal and a commitment. Make connecting with people who aren't your family or workmates a Level-1 priority.

As we discussed earlier, this will be harder than you think, both practically and philosophically. You're busy. You're already exhausted and you already have too many things going on. You feel like you don't have time for another "thing." And our culture is constantly pushing us to think as individuals. *My* home. *My* day. *My* job. *My* dreams. *My* future. *My* stuff. It's etched into the fabric of our founding documents. You have the right to life, liberty, and the pursuit of happiness. It's mine. Alone. My world revolves around me.

This is a recipe for death.

Decide you're going to do it. Decide you're going to make the effort to make friends.

2. Look for shared experiences.

Leagues, teams, community programs, theater, shooting competitions—seek out shared experiences. Go hunting or fishing with someone. Invite a few guys to a concert or a ball game. Take a class at a local community college. Actually go to your church small group and then invite folks out afterward. Start a running club, a book club, or start lifting with a few like-minded folks. Dust off the old guitar and the old Marshall amp and invite some guys over to jam.

Or maybe you have old friends you'd like to reconnect with. People you shared experiences with in years gone by. Maybe old high school or college friends. Old workmates or people you used to hang out with at the former church you attended. Dig into various social media platforms and see if any of your old crew lives in your area.

I don't care what it is or who it is or from what era of your life you found them. Just start.

Be intentional. Make time. This is life or death.

3. Go first and extend hospitality.

This is one of the Delony Family Core Values. We love having people over. Even when things are messy and I haven't mowed the lawn.[97] Invite people over to your place, even if it's not fancy. Even if it's a one-bedroom apartment. Or go out and pick up the tab. Invite folks and their kids to the park. I started this chapter with the story of me literally asking adult human beings if they would be my friend. That wasn't the first time, and I'm sure it won't be the last time. I asked them while they were sitting around my kitchen table.

Just ask. Other people are desperate for relationship and connection too. It's not just you and me. But somebody has to go first. Somebody has to break through the barriers and the discomfort and the uncertainty and just make something happen. Let it be you.

- "Can we get together this week?"
- "Let's go grab a drink."
- "Y'all want to go eat after the game?"

---

97. This is an inside joke among my friends. I'm always trying to mow before company arrives, and I'm generally running late. So when friends come over, they usually watch me finish mowing for a while before we all hang out. I'm working on it.

- "I got an extra ticket."
- "I'm taking my kids to the park. You should join us."

Will it be weird? Yes, but probably not as much as you think.

Could it be awkward? For sure.

Is it possible the people you ask will say no? Absolutely . . . and rejection is brutal.

But go first anyway.

Is it possible you'll get together with someone and it will be just "okay" and you'll both realize you weren't meant to be lifelong friends? Yep.

Do it anyway.

Find people in your life right now that you can ask to join you for something. And don't be dramatic about it. Be chill. Be direct. Be your weird, glorious, wacky self. If not just one person, get a group and invite several people.

Extend hospitality and go first.

4. Say yes to invitations and adventures.

This is another of the Delony Family Core Values. We do our best to always say yes. If we can afford it and we can fit it in, we're up for it. Camping, puppet shows, hunting trips, punk rock *and* country music concerts, gardening groups, fishing, hiking, roofing, mowing, and cleaning out a home that got destroyed in a natural disaster. Whatever, whenever. The answer is *yes*.

Shared experiences—especially trials, teamwork, or challenges—unite and bond people together. When possible, say yes.

When I started taking a hard look at my own loneliness, I realized I always deleted the invite texts and emails. I skipped the work socials. I didn't join the softball team, and I bowed out of the karaoke dive bar.

And I complained about not having any friends. All of us have done this.

- "Want to grab some coffee?"
- "Dude, we're all going for drinks . . . come with us."
- "We're roadtripping to see the Avett Brothers and then an Astros game. You're coming!"
- "You hate golf too? Good . . . you're coming hunting with us."

Go. Do. Stop hiding. Stand up. Get on with it, whatever it is. Just say yes to adventures.[98]

5. Get out of your house and go where other people are.

It sounds simple, but if you want to get connected with other people—or expand and deepen your current pool of friendships—you're going to have to leave your home and go where other people are gathered.

Yes, you heard me right. You have to leave your house. Turn off the screens. Stop bingeing. Be intentional about being around people. In this scenario, you don't have to do any planning or recruiting. You just show up.

I don't know what's going to work best for you, but I know there are lots of options. Sign up for a membership at the local rec center and play some ball a few mornings a week. Take ju-jitsu. Join a band. Or a yoga class. Pick a hobby that involves groups instead of individuals. Get involved at your church. Go to a park. Go to some parties. Do lunch in the school cafeteria with other moms or dads.

Just go where people are.

---

98. It goes without saying to not put yourself in unsafe or dangerous situations. Be wise and smart and not an idiot. But otherwise, say YES!

6. Find people to serve.

Take walks in your neighborhood and pick up trash. Grab one of your kids and make lunches for your homeless neighbors, and then go hand them out. Do a family shift at a food bank. Bake all day and take cookies to your neighbors. Volunteer.

Do things to build connections within your community. As my friend Andy Gullahorn says, "Love local." Serve your street, your neighborhood, your town.

Again, the idea is relatively simple. You have a lot of gifts as an individual, and by extension as a couple or a family. You've got resources, financial and otherwise. You have skills, talents, and abilities. Most of us at the very least have a strong back and working arms. These are all resources that can be invested as a way of improving the community where you live.

Want to be really out there? When you do find a place to serve, invite other people to join you.

Volunteer to do some landscaping at the entrance to your neighborhood and invite your other neighbors to join you. Have tacos delivered and maybe even grab a drink afterward. Visiting inmates through a prison ministry? Invite a co-worker or a dad from your son's baseball team.

What Next?

Once you're around people and making connections, it's time to go deeper. When you start hanging out with a few new friends, it might be tempting to keep things safe, floating on the surface.

Fight the urge to stay on the surface or be a creepy over-sharer when you just meet someone. Remember, friendship is a skill that you can practice and improve. This means you don't have to wait for some magical "click." You can take active steps to cultivate and deepen key relationships on your own. Sometimes this happens naturally, which is awesome. Sometimes things just flow with a friend or group of friends in ways that are effortless. You like hanging out.

But sometimes it doesn't happen that way.

It's okay if friendships don't work out. Everyone is not for everyone. Remember that your identity cannot be tethered to making people like you. This makes you codependent and bonkers. Remember too that there are seasons when people are legitimately busy and cannot spend a lot of time together. In other seasons, you can hang out all the time. As much as possible, keep things consistent—it keeps everyone accountable to the relationship.

To go deeper, be intentional about leaning into the friend characteristics I mentioned earlier.

1. *Tell your friends about the good stuff.* When you're excited or amped up about something cool that just happened, make a call, send a text, and spread the good news. You go first.

2. *Tell your friends about the bad stuff.* When there's something difficult going down, don't keep it to yourself. Tell your friends what's happening and how it makes you feel. Don't overdo it—you can wear people out by being the central hub of drama. All friends won't be able to come to your aid every single time for every single need, and that's okay. Every relationship needs boundaries. But if you need something, ask.

3. *Tell your friends what hurts.* When you open up about the struggles that have defined you, you'll help others understand you on a much deeper level and you'll give your friends an opportunity to find the same freedom. Be smart, safe, and socially aware with this type of sharing. Make sure

the setting is right. Understand that not everyone has the tools to handle this type of heavy news. A therapist does therapy and long-term trauma care. A good friend hugs you, cries with you, and brings flowers or dinner or a few fishing poles.

4. *Be honest.* Tell the truth. When people say or do something you don't like, or especially something that hurts your feelings—say so. Say something. Give them a chance to show you that they can be trusted. Give them a chance to say they're sorry. And never, ever send these messages via text or social media. Write a letter (or ugh . . . an email) if you have to. But if at all possible, call or visit in person to talk things through.

5. *Show up.* This is the most important thing. Friends don't just talk about being there when things get hard—they actually go. Friends show up at funerals. Every time. They check on your kids when things get tough. They come over when the doctor says "cancer." You don't have to know what to say or bring or do. Just show up.

When you do these things consistently over time, your friendships will become a force of strength and security. They will become solid, like concrete.

I know this chapter has been basic for many of us. It felt weird even writing it. But we need it. We're failing. We're all alone, and our bodies and families and hearts are paying a heavy price.

You are worth being loved.

You're worth having people in your life who you don't have to clean the house for or put on makeup for. You're worth having friends you don't have to be loud with, lie to, or suck in your gut around. You're worth openness, truth-telling, and honesty.

Build relationships. Invest in them. Prioritize them. Make the call. Keep showing up. Say yes.

Get connected.

CHAPTER 11

Change Your Thoughts

D r. Hendricks sat down in his chair and announced to the class: "Time for a case study . . . but this time you're the case."

I was in a doctoral counseling class, and we were all sitting in a wonky-looking circle, chairs facing inward toward each other. Dr. Hendricks was famous for his case studies.

"Suppose you've been meeting with a client for six months. They come every week without fail. They tell the truth, they show up on time, and they do the homework assignments. They're a good client and they have been diligent in trying to learn and grow. Then one day the client comes into your office with a lot of anger. When you ask what's wrong, they let you have it.

"'For starters' your client says, 'you suck at counseling. I've given you something like $2,500 over the past six months, and everything is worse. I tried your little talk-to-your-boss idea, and not only did I not get the raise, but I got demoted. My boyfriend still ended up moving out, and I haven't lost any weight. I put my trust in you, and you let me down. You shouldn't have taken my money and you shouldn't be a therapist.'"

The professor looked around at each of the fifteen or so people in the room. "How would you respond?"

Woah. I had only been counseling real clients for a few months. The sessions were very personal, deep, and raw. The thought of a client telling me that I sucked was heavy.

I raised my hand and spoke up. "That would probably kill me."

My professor dug in. "Why would that kill you? Tell me more."

I responded: "My counseling sessions have been intimate," I answered. "My clients have told me their fears, their loves and sexual habits; they've talked about their hurts and the hurdles they're trying to overcome. I feel close to these people. If one of them came in and dropped that bomb, I think it would crush me."

One of my classmates spoke up. She was a brilliant and wise counselor with more than twenty years of experience.

"No, John," she said. "They don't get that."

"What do you mean, 'They don't get that?'" I chuckled. "Is that some counselor-lingo nonsense?"

What my classmate said next changed my life. It helped my marriage, my friendships, and my spiritual life. What she said changed *me.*

"Your clients don't get that type of access to you. They don't have permission to hurt you. *You decide who gets to hurt your feelings, John.*"

I laughed and rolled my eyes, but inside I felt flushed. Alarmed. Defense mechanisms were kicking in. *No way.*

She kept going: "You get to decide who hurts your feelings. You get to decide who pierces your heart, frustrates you, and annoys you. People can take away your livelihood, your possessions, and even your life—but you get to choose who hurts you. Not your clients."

"So it's like my heart is a little box," I said, poking at her a little bit, "and I get to choose who I allow in it? It sounds so cute."

"Exactly," Lisa answered, not laughing back. "You choose."

"How many people can go in the box?

"I don't know. Maybe four. At most five."

I laughed again, but it was all a show. What she said was already boring a hole deep into my inner core. As I rode my bike home from class, I thought about putting a box on the kitchen table and putting names of actual people inside. Which four or five people would I put in the box? Who would I allow to hurt my feelings?

I have lots of acquaintances, friends, family, and colleagues scattered across the country.

I tried to reverse-engineer the question: Who was I allowing to hurt my feelings right now?

My blood ran cold.

Everyone.

I let everyone hurt my feelings.

I had given everyone access to my heart. Students, teachers, family members, my little kids, plus years of friends, acquaintances, and co-workers. I let people I didn't even know or care about on the internet get me riled up. News anchors I would never meet in person made me angry. I still had old girlfriends' voices rattling around in my chest. And I let preachers, teachers, neighbors, and politicians drive me bonkers.

By the time I cruised into my driveway at home, I realized I had between two thousand and a million people crammed into that box. I was a punching bag for other people's opinions.

I had mistaken wholehearted living for open-access living. I had no boundaries.

Right then and there, I started taking people out of the box.

I took my infant children out of the box *because they are children.* I should not allow children to hurt me. They are not built to carry that type of responsibility.

I took out my parents and in-laws. I love them and they are wonderful—but I realized I was responsible for my life and for co-creating my marriage and my life with my wife. Our parents didn't get a vote.

I took out my bosses, fellow Little League dads, and anyone I was only digitally tethered to. I took out anyone on the television, people I had not spoken to in years, and old elementary school friends that I didn't know anymore. I kept going, taking more and more people out.

I left my wife in the box. A couple of very close friends. A few mentors and a spiritual advisor. Ultimately I got down to six people, and that's about where it remains today. I have given six people access to my deepest self. I have given six people permission to hurt me. It was a transcendent experience. I was set free.

By the way, I called or wrote each of those six people and let them know they had permission to speak into my life, and I would listen. I gave them permission to hurt me, and I asked them to wield that power gently, boldly, and with wisdom.

I have never been more at peace with the world, even as it is fracturing and reorganizing right under my feet. I have never slept better, and I have never had more energy to serve and love and be present with everyone, from strangers to loved ones.

Why was this such a big revelation for me? Why was it so helpful and transformational? Because I realized that if I get to choose *who* hurts me, I also could choose *what* hurts me. Or bothers me. Or makes me angry.

I realized that I get to choose what's happening in my brain: who and what has access to it, what I spend time thinking about, who I spend time thinking about. I get to choose to meditate on the scary things or search for beautiful things. I can't always choose my feelings, but I get to choose my *thoughts about how I feel.*

Before that moment, I'd always felt at the mercy of my own spinning brain. I thought I was a victim of my thoughts. In fact, *I thought I was my thoughts.* I thought I was my good thoughts, my bad thoughts, and my warped thoughts. I thought my life was to be lived in response to my worst-case scenarios, my pessimistic outlooks, and the countless imaginary conversations that I was always having in my mind, but that I would never have in real life.

I was on the frontier of a new personal reality.

I had been introduced to a new, deeper type of ownership.

I am in control of what goes in my head, and I am in control of what stays in my head. I get to choose my thoughts.

You Get to Decide What You Think

Remember, we are changing our lives. We are dealing with the bricks in our backpacks and setting them down. We are seeking to live well and to live whole lives that are more joyful and peaceful, more patient and kind, more powerful and strong. To change your life, you first have to:

1. Own your stories.
2. Acknowledge your reality.
3. Get connected in meaningful relationships.

The next thing you must do is *change your thoughts.* This is the fourth step to wellness.

We have all experienced the voices in our head that never stop chattering. We're constantly talking to ourselves—narrating, approving, justifying, and judging. If this voice was a friend or a roommate, we'd hit him in the mouth. If it was a radio or television, we'd turn it off. But since we think it's *us* talking to us, we let it ride.

Our brain is full of thoughts. All day, every day.

But just because a thought pops into your mind doesn't mean you should keep thinking about it.

David Kessler says, "Every day we choose our thoughts. As a society, we don't have much awareness of that. *We have to unlearn the belief that we have no power over what happens in our minds.*"[99]

Yes. You choose the thoughts you think.

Our thoughts are the pictures and the voices in our heads that never stop talking. Without tools or practices to stop the noise or dismiss the pictures, they continue. Always going. Always on a loop. Left untended, they slash and burn everything.

But they can be wrangled and controlled.

The first thing you must realize in order to change your thoughts is that *you decide what you think.*

Kessler wrote of this in his masterwork *Finding Meaning: The Sixth Stage of Grief.* In the book, Kessler details an exercise he uses when working with parents who have lost a child. Parents who lose a child are often paralyzed by visions of their child in the hospital, in a casket, or in pain.[100] These devastatingly intrusive thoughts take a parent's mind captive and play on repeat year after year after year. The parents' brains remain on high alert, never wanting Mom or Dad to forget the horror, so that they will always remember to vigilantly avoid a similar fate.

As if they could forget.

But Kessler teaches grieving parents that they can indeed control their thoughts. He asks them to close their eyes and imagine

---

99. Kessler, *Finding Meaning*, 72–73. Emphasis mine.

100. When I did crisis work with the police department, it was often my job to keep parents from seeing their children or teens who had just died. It was always best for them for the last memories of their kids to be positive or happy ones, and not the harsh, visual realities of tragic last moments.

a purple elephant in their mind.[101] Just sitting there wearing a cute little yellow hat.

You try it. Do it right now.

Close your eyes and picture a purple elephant wearing a little yellow hat. The elephant can be sitting or standing, it doesn't matter. Just get a good clear picture of the elephant in your mind.

In your mind's eye, can you see a picture of a purple elephant wearing a little yellow hat?

Well, there you go.

You just proved to yourself that you can control your thoughts.

You chose to see the elephant in your mind. And you can choose everything else as well.

You can decide what to think about. What to focus on. Whether to be curious or to judge. How to interpret and implement.

When that thought pops into your head of your old boyfriend who hurt you, your wife who cheated on you, that teacher who cussed at your kid, or the final image of your mom at the funeral home...

You have control.

The same with thoughts about endless news violence, war, climate concerns, the economy, your faith questions, your phobias, trauma memories, or that guy who flipped you off in line at Astroworld twenty-eight years ago. (I still can't believe I just walked away from him.)

Most people believe that our thoughts just occur randomly, like bolts of lightning. And we do get struck by bolts of lightning. The picture of our husband with an old girlfriend or of our kids staring down at an empty plate can flash into our minds unannounced.

---

101. Kessler, *Finding Meaning*, 73.

But from that moment on, we choose whether we meditate on the thought or let it breeze on by.

And yes, I said breeze on by. Just letting it go.

It's vitally important for us to remember that we get to choose what to think. Why? Because our thoughts are real. I don't mean "real" in the sense of being "true" (although that may be the case). I mean "real" as in they are physical. Your thoughts are created and sustained within your brain as electrical impulses, which means they exist in a physical space. Hormones and synapses and electricity are firing and connecting and creating. Dr. Caroline Leaf has said it this way: "Thoughts are real things. And, like real things, they generate energy: little packets of energy called photons, which are the fundamental particles of light."[102]

Your thoughts are particles of light. They have mass. They impact your biophysiological responses. They signal your heart to beat faster. They signal your armpits to sweat, your face to get hot, and adrenaline and cortisol to flood your system. Or they signal your body to power down. To depress. To loop and cycle and numb, numb, numb.

Thoughts are real things that have real consequences. They will run on autopilot until you're ready to take them back.

Remember the bricks in your backpack? The stories we're born into, that we're told, that really happened, and the stories we tell ourselves?

The stories are thoughts. For sure, they can also reside in our bodies as trauma and stored energy, but when you set about tracing them back to their source, you'll find your stories primarily exist as

---

102. Dr. Caroline Leaf, *Cleaning Up Your Mental Mess: 5 Simple, Scientifically Proven Steps to Reduce Anxiety, Stress, and Toxic Thinking,* (Grand Rapids: Baker Books, 2021), 158.

thoughts. In your mind. We rehash them and re-experience them in an attempt to protect ourselves. Thinking about worst-case scenarios and harmful memories and betrayals feels like we're keeping ourselves safe.

But most of the time, there's no real, immediate threat.

Rumination is an utter waste of your time. It's just not going to work. It's like using a hammer to saw through a plank of wood. It's the wrong tool for any job.

Let's pick up some new tools.

You Have to Be Intentional About Your Inputs

The second thing to do in order to control your thoughts is to be intentional and discerning about what you allow in your brain. I know, I know. I sound like an old-man dad who is trying to find hidden Satanic messages on your Ozzy Osbourne albums or who won't let you watch PG-13 movies until you're actually thirteen. (I grew up in a house like that.)

But it's true.

I can't tell you how many people I talk with on a regular basis who work stressful jobs, who go home to chaos with kids and stressful marriages, and who also consume a steady streaming diet of murder podcasts, social media drama, and *Law and Order: Special Victim's Unit* reruns. Endless 24/7 cycles of death, famine, and destruction are destructive to your biology. To your spirit. To your mind.

It's like injecting cancer directly into your pancreas and wondering why you don't feel good.

During the years I was laid low by crippling anxiety and depression, I spent most of my waking hours reading doomsday reports on the bleak future of higher education, the collapse of global mental health, and the crumbling of the US economy. When I wasn't scanning those cheery news items, I was reading about climate science, drought, and post-apocalyptic fiction.[103] Also, this was around the time the Showtime serial-killer soap opera *Dexter* was released. I was angry, frazzled, and spewing my opinions and vitriol everywhere.

Dr. Andrew Weil, Director of Integrative Medicine at the University of Arizona, recommends that people be conscious of and intentional about their choices of media, especially news shows and other sources designed to make you angry or anxious. Dr. Weil advocates for news fasts, limiting screen time and television shows, and being mindful of how certain types of media impact your body and your thoughts. I have dramatically changed my media consumption choices, and it has made a remarkable difference.

This is not about ignoring the bad and the evil in the world. Not one bit. I know it's there. I swim in it for a living. I am always checking in with real people and real data. And I also understand that it can be a privilege to be able to turn it off. But I rarely, rarely watch ugliness or darkness for entertainment anymore. I don't scroll and read endlessly devastating news stories. I have friends in the military who will let me know if the apocalypse is upon us. I get the information I need; I pay special attention to things I can impact and support in my local community; and then I turn it off.

You cannot solve every global crisis. You have to stop throwing punches at everything, because you're not hitting anything and you're exhausted.

I'm also intentional about the music I listen to, most of the movies I watch, and the books I consume.

---

103. I'll never forget reading Cormac McCarthy's *The Road* the week my son was born. In the middle of spinning out. I had no idea what it was about. I literally just picked it up. *The Road* is a phenomenal book . . . but I should have been reading something more optimistic, like *Pet Cemetery* or the Hunger Games trilogy.

I'm on a relentless, never-ending search for beauty. I look to consume the good things in life—of which there are many. I spend as much time as possible in nature.[104]

Years later, I fall asleep on most nights without drugs. I rarely get upset, and when I do, I have tools to cope with it both immediately and in the long term. I'm intentional about breathing. About exercise. About my diet (except when I'm in Houston or San Antonio, and then the wheels come off because I'm a sucker for true Mexican food). About being kind and patient and choosing to look for solutions. I don't miss sunsets or early mornings very often. Stars are beautiful again. I laugh with family and friends.

As much as I am able, I am intentional about what goes in my head on a regular basis.

And it has made all the difference.

Be Intentional About Your Thoughts

The third thing you need to know about taking control of your thoughts is that it will require intentionality. Changing your thought patterns isn't going to happen without effort. Some people meditate, some take on a yoga practice. Others journal their thoughts out of their heads and onto the page. Some fake it till you make it—they just start "acting" in an intended or preferred way until their mind catches up.

In the beginning, working at your thoughts can be difficult, frustrating, and exhausting. When I first started, it was maddening. I had so many thoughts flying around at any given moment that anytime I sat still, I felt like I was under attack.

---

104. A number of scientific studies have connected time in nature to better mental health outcomes.

Mo Gawdat says that "so much of your happiness depends not on the conditions of the world around you but on the thoughts you create about them. . . . When you learn to calmly observe the dialogue and the drama . . . , you can watch your thoughts, knowing the only power they can gain over you is the power you grant them."[105]

I always believed that being intentional in this area meant I would never have negative or dark thoughts, and if I did, I wasn't well or whole yet. This is incorrect. Renewing your mind is a daily practice, something you keep coming back to over and over. Intentionality is a choice and a skill you can develop.

But intentionality is difficult, especially in the beginning. In fact, it can be brutal. Once you start paying close attention to the thoughts tossing around in your mind, it can feel overwhelming. There are just too many. They're so negative, or dirty, or unrealistic, or depressing.

This is why most people do life unconsciously—or as Ellen Langer calls it, "mindlessly." They're on autopilot. They are happy to outsource their thoughts and feelings. Because at first, this intentionality is *work*. It's exhausting. In the beginning, it doesn't feel worth it. It's how people live without a budget, without professional goals, and without a picture for how their marriages could look. It seems easier to avoid your thoughts until it's not.

Being intentional is hard because we have to make decisions about the things we will think about and the things we won't think about. We have to make decisions about our identity.

Intentionality asks: Is this helping me move toward who I want to be?

---

105. Mo Gawdat, *Solve for Happy: Engineer Your Path to Joy*, (New York: North Star Way, 2017), 72.

For most of us, it's easier to not even think about this question, especially if our old hurts inform how we identify ourselves.

For example, consider someone who regularly thinks, *I'm ugly and nobody will ever want to get close to me. No one would ever want to kiss this face.* Is that true? Probably not. But if I believe it's true, then every time someone looks at me, I will assume they are disgusted by my looks and thinking of a reason to get away from me.

And soon I will assume that everyone is disgusted by my looks: My dad. And those kids in seventh grade. And, since I had no dates in high school or college, every one of those guys or girls who wasn't already in a relationship.

And now our negative thoughts are off to the races. Our brain is filled with them. The cortisol and adrenaline are flowing. Our bodies are geared up, and our thoughts are our shield. If we were to let those thoughts go, we would have to open ourselves to the possibility of making new connections and finding intimacy—which would also mean opening up to the possibility of being rejected and feeling hurt. So we choose to keep the thoughts that are comfortable even though they are harmful.

We remind ourselves: He left us. She cheated. You got fired before and you'll probably get fired again. You don't make enough money. Your people can't get ahead. You're not smart enough. We become convinced that our boss hates us. That our co-worker is trying to sabotage us. That our neighbor has it out for us. That we'll never have a lot of money.

We are awash in negative thinking. Past thinking. Protective thinking. Prohibitive thinking.

And we keep carrying the bricks for another mile. And another mile.

Kessler addresses our approach this way: "Imagine the thoughts in your mind as being like a garden. Whatever thoughts you water are the thoughts that will grow. When you have a horrible image in your mind, if you keep looking at it and telling yourself that you can't stop, that image will become stronger and stronger."[106]

The really great news is that the same principle is true for good thoughts and good stories. When we water and nurture *those*, they will grow into a larger part of our identity.

So if you want to change your thoughts, you have to be intentional about letting the old ones go. The thoughts that kept you safe in the past—but that now suffocate you in the present. When there is just one nasty meta-thought that consumes you? You have to be intentional. When you have a million maddening thoughts swirling around like a tornado? You have to be intentional about stopping them. And you have to be intentional about replacing them with new thoughts.

It's going to take time. You don't develop the skill of rejecting harmful thoughts overnight. Same for accepting and cultivating positive thoughts.

This is hard and you need to give yourself plenty of chances to practice. When you have negative thoughts, explore them. With each line of thought, ask yourself, "What is this trying to protect me from?" Work to replace it. And do this over and over again until it automates in a new direction.

Here's my challenge to you: give yourself sixty to ninety days. That's two or three months of actively and intentionally training your thoughts.

Remember the purple elephant. You can think of different things. You can choose your thoughts. I'll walk you through that next.

---

106. Kessler, *Finding Meaning*, 73.

How to Change Your Thoughts

Let's get down to the actual mechanics of how to control your thoughts. As I mentioned, it can be tedious and slow at first. But with time, it becomes something you do automatically. Here's how I do it:

Write Down Your Thoughts

The very first thing in changing your thoughts is to become aware of them. You do this by writing them down.

Similar to writing down your stories, writing down your thoughts creates distance from them, allowing you to see them objectively and gain perspective over them. Jocko Willink calls it detaching. Michael Singer calls this being mindful. Whatever you call it, the result is the same. When thoughts are whirling in our minds, or when they're running automated in the background, they control us.

Out on the paper, our thoughts are under our control.

Here are some thoughts that might pop into your head:

- *I'm just a loser.*
- *I'll always be an alcoholic.*
- *I can't help being late.*
- *I keep thinking of kissing her, and I'm married to someone else.*
- *That guy in the car in front of me is trying to kill us all.*
- *I have to hit him back.*

As we talked about, when thoughts and pictures like these come into our minds, we have a choice. Are we going to water them or uproot them and replace them with something else?

When an unwanted thought pops into your head, write it down.

If what pops into your head is both disturbing and true, then you have a puzzle to begin solving. Be curious. Like having a hard conversation you've been avoiding.

And remember: this isn't a one-time event. Writing down your thoughts is a lifelong practice, like making a budget or exercising. I keep a small notebook with me at all times for just this purpose. I write my thoughts down and decide if they're serving me well. If you choose to live a well, whole life, you will do this (or something similar) for the rest of your life.

Over time, you will begin to link these thoughts to the stories you wrote down. To your bricks. Over time, you will begin to see how your thoughts grew out of your bricks, like weeds in a sidewalk. The more you write them down and get some space between you and your thoughts, the more control you have over them.

Listen to Your Body and Feel Your Feelings

As you write down your thoughts, pay special attention to your body. Listen for what it's telling you.

For example, what physical sensations do you experience as you contemplate a specific story? Is there a pressure in your chest? A sharp pain in your shoulder or your wrist? Does your heart start to race or your breathing get shallow? We store physical sensations in our bodies, connected to memories, which means our thoughts often come to us with physical responses.

We call them *feelings* for a reason.

What happens inside when you consider your thoughts in connection to the stories you wrote down? Are you instantly ready for a fight? Do you suddenly need to GET OUT OF HERE? Do you feel danger? Overload—time to get into bed and crawl under the covers?

- Does anger rise up? Are you starting to feel trapped?
- Is your brain spiraling into anxiety?
- Do you want to go eat? Or call someone?
- Grab a drink or a smoke?
- Go lift weights? Hit something?
- Do you feel shame or guilt?

Are you starting to think about numbing out? Do you have a strong urge to grab your weighted blanket and re-watch a couple seasons of *The Office*?

Listen and feel what your body is doing as it deals with the pain, trauma, or strong emotions connected to the thoughts and stories.

By the way, don't reach for that cigarette or TV remote. We'll talk about this more in the next chapter, but these are opportunities to consciously let go of your body's defense mechanisms and make healthier and more productive choices.

Demand Evidence

Now that we have our thoughts down on paper, it's time to flip the script on them. Instead of them controlling you, *it's time for you to take control.*

Your list of stories, thoughts, and feelings might look something like this:

Figure 1

1. *THOUGHTS: I've got giant bags under my eyes. My butt is sagging off. I'm ugly and overweight. My husband's co-worker is more attractive than me. He probably wishes he could be with her instead of me. He might leave like my dad did.*

BODY RESPONSE: My stomach drops. My heart starts racing and I feel a little mad and nauseous at the same time. I just feel hollow. And yuck. And that this isn't fair. I'm getting back in bed.

Figure 2

2. *THOUGHTS: The economy is falling apart as we speak. I need to cash out my retirement. I check my phone right when I wake up to see what happened while I was sleeping. I let my kids watch TV because they think I'm lame anyway and I'm just exhausted. I can't believe I've got gray hair now . . . none of the other teachers my age have gray hair.*

BODY RESPONSE: Jittery. Lots of movement. I'm just mad. I feel like my body is frumpy. I want to go get some of the ice cream that's left in the fridge. It wouldn't take much for me to cry, but that would be dumb.

Sometimes you become aware of your thoughts the other way around. You find yourself reaching for the ice cream with one hand while holding the remote in the other. Or you find yourself about to hit Send on a rageful email and you take one quick moment to pause. What thoughts are racing through your mind about anger or worthiness? About your need to numb? What are your mind and body trying to protect you from?

Once you start putting together this kind of list, and once you've made a commitment to hearing what your body wants to say, it's time to demand evidence of the thoughts and stories you've written down.

The big question you want to address with this step is: *Are your thoughts true?* Does this specific story (and the thoughts connected with it) have any basis in reality?

I want you to look at your thoughts and demand evidence. Are they true?

Sometimes they are flat-out false.

Or they feel right, but you have no proof.

Other times, things get complicated. We have to sift through some layers. Like with the thought "I'm ugly and overweight." This is subjective, but is there any evidence to support the thought? That's not a fun idea, I know, but if those thoughts have been pressing down on you for years—maybe even decades—it's worth digging in to see what may or may not be true.

For example, has a doctor diagnosed you as overweight? Have you had to buy new clothes? Do you have a friend or a counselor who will help you be objective? Or are you comparing yourself to Instagram models, curated Facebook influencers, and contestants on *The Bachelorette*? Have you and your spouse stopped being intimate and you've told yourself the story that it's because of your looks? Or maybe your spouse told you the lack of intimacy is because you're ugly and overweight.

Where are the thoughts coming from?

And your husband's co-worker. Is this true? Have you talked to your husband? Have you told him that you're feeling vulnerable and in the shadow of his colleague? Or do you remain silent, slowly building up resentment and anger?

Again, this is one set of thoughts. They could be true. They could be completely false. They could be a little of each.

The point is, when you get them out of your brain and on paper, you can regain control. You can dismiss the lies and confront the truths head-on.

Often when we demand evidence of our thoughts, we find they are riddled with nonsense. Sure, you gained twenty pounds over the past five years. But you're not ugly and unlovable. Your husband doesn't want to leave you just because he has an attractive co-worker. Or maybe he does want to leave you.

Where you find out that your story is true, we will address what to do in the next chapter. If you find evidence that your story is false—or if you fail to find any evidence that it's true—you're ready for the next step.

Set the Bricks Down

Changing your thoughts is about intentionally letting go of false or incomplete thoughts and exchanging them with truth and meaning.

This is where it becomes apparent that a lot of your thoughts and stories have merged into a toxic mess. You start pulling on the threads of your thoughts and you realize they grew out of stories you've been telling yourself for a long time. When you realize you're carrying a story that's false, decide that you want to set it down. Stop trying to reverse-engineer why your dad left you. We know it wasn't because of the snacks—and truth be known, you'll probably never know why he left.

Stop hauling that brick around with you everywhere you go. Set. It. Down.

Be done.

Any choice to keep repeating that story or carry it further *is a choice to be more miserable*. It's a choice to have less joy. It's a choice to hate more.

Drop the bricks.

Not only that, reject any thoughts that stem from those stories. Remember what we explored earlier about intentionality. Even when you've identified a story as false, your mind will keep trying to dredge up the thoughts and feelings connected with that story simply because of momentum. You're in a mental rut. You've probably been spinning that story for a long time. You have to be intentional about choosing which thoughts are allowed in your mind—and which thoughts are rejected.

Sometimes when my mind takes off on me, I'll say NO! really loud. I can be out on a run, in the shower, or just walking through the living room.

My family knows what's going on when I do this. I'll shout just that one word—"Nope!"—and keep walking, not talking to anyone except myself.

My wife thinks it's hilarious.

Why do I do this? Because I've identified a thought that I don't want in my head, that has been proven false, and I choose to get rid of it. "Nope!" And then I have a series of other thoughts ready to go in its place.

This part is equally important. You don't just stop thinking a thought. Part of setting down a brick is replacing the old story with a new one.

Maybe the economy *is* on the verge of a recession. *That's why I have a fully funded emergency fund.*

Maybe my wife doesn't like how I've been leaving my clothes in a pile when I get home from a work trip. *But she's not going to leave me. And I can choose to be better about putting my clothes in the laundry.*

When the picture of your son at the funeral home zaps into your mind, gracefully let the thought pass by, intentionally remembering a time when he was riding his Big Wheel and you all were laughing your heads off.

When your boss asks you to swing by her office, and she cc's HR on the email, and your body immediately responds as though you're getting fired . . . intentionally breathe, drop your shoulders, and remind yourself: you are a valued member of your organization, you contribute financial and social capital, and you are probably getting called in to get a promotion. Or maybe you are getting fired and you need to focus on the specific details of what comes next. Flying into a panic or a rage will only make things worse.

You'll figure out a system that works for you, but what you must do in order to change your thoughts is refuse to waste any more mental energy on thoughts you've determined are untrue.

Stop lying to yourself and others. Put the bricks down.

Before we go further, let's pause. I can feel some of you thinking: *This is so stupid. If I could just control my thoughts, I would. This guy is an idiot.*

Here's your moment! Challenge that thought that you can't control your thoughts. That you can't take control of your mind. That through practice—whether meditation, intensive work with a counselor, daily journaling and gratitude practices, or intentionality about what you watch, read, and listen to—

you can't change everything.

Because you can.

As we transition to the end of this section, you'll begin to see the lines blur between controlling your thoughts and controlling your actions. You'll feel your new thoughts becoming your new stories. This is natural and right. Technically, controlling your thoughts *is* an action. You have to control your thoughts to get your body to move.

The final two parts to controlling your thoughts are about changing your mindset. This will unlock the chains that you believed others had bound you in.

These steps—forgiveness and control—are your keys to freedom.

Forgive Others and Yourself

I know you don't want to. Sometimes it feels so good to hang on to injustice, past wrongs, or the times you just know you were right. Especially when the person or people who hurt you won't apologize.

Or maybe you're the one who screwed up. And you've sentenced yourself to a lifetime of abusive language and self-hatred.

Either way, if you want to be well, you have to forgive.

If you've been the victim of abuse, trauma, or systemic injustice, forgiveness can feel like quitting. Like giving up and rolling over. Like saying that what they did or what they're doing wasn't so bad or it doesn't matter.

No.

Forgiveness is a bold and brave display of power.

Choosing not to forgive someone is like poisoning yourself and hoping that other person will die.

Forgiveness isn't about other people.

Forgiveness is about you.

Forgiveness is looking directly into the eyes and hearts and spirits of those who hurt you and saying, "I refuse to carry your hate or pain for another step." It sets you free from bitterness and from the pain of re-experiencing traumatic memories over and over again. Forgiveness lightens your load.

And it helps you get your life back.

So forgive them for what they said.

Forgive them for what they didn't say.

Forgive them for what they did.

Forgive them for what they neglected or refused to do.

It's right to be angry, scared, pissed off, and sometimes filled with rage. It's normal to feel those things.

But then set the day and say, "I'm not carrying this anymore. I'm not giving you space in my backpack, my head, or my heart any longer." Say, "I forgive you. I'm out."

If you can offer that forgiveness in person, on the phone, or through a note, that's great. "Dad, I forgive you for leaving." "Mom, I forgive you for not protecting me; I know he was hurting you too."

If you can't offer forgiveness in person—whether it would be harmful to you or the individual in question is no longer alive—it's okay to simply express forgiveness out loud: "You were supposed to be a blessing in my life as a priest, but instead you abused me for years. I'm not carrying you, your evil, or your stories with me anymore. I forgive you."

Forgiveness does not mean that you don't pursue justice. It doesn't mean that you skip calling the police. Forgiveness doesn't mean that you don't report what happened to your HR director. Forgiveness simply means you will no longer carry those who hurt you in your thoughts, heart, body, or spirit.

Now for the really tricky part: sometimes the person you need to forgive is *you*. We all have those moments and those memories that make it necessary to forgive ourselves.

The same principles apply. If there are ways you harmed yourself or packed your life with negative stories, you have to forgive yourself. Forgive what you did or didn't do. Forgive what you said or failed to say. Speak that forgiveness out loud again and again.

"John, I forgive you for spending so many years chasing success instead of wellness."

"John, I forgive you for treating your wife less than she deserved. Or for missing Hank's game for a work meeting. Or for yelling at the driver in front of you after lecturing your daughter on the importance of self-control."

"John, I forgive you for pushing that girl in fourth grade. John, I forgive you for lying and stealing so much when you were a kid. John, I forgive you for not always honoring your parents."

You try it.

When you do, you may wake up tomorrow and find the bricks back in your bag. Forgive again. Keep forgiving until you wake up one morning with a song.

Only keep those thoughts that are true and good and helpful.

Control What You Can Control

He said it.

She left.

He never came back home.

The economy crashed.

You gained the weight.

They treated you differently.

You texted back.

You have six figures of credit card debt.

And what happens next is *all that you can control.*

To change your thoughts, you must own this:

You cannot edit, change, or have a do-over for the past. Not for what was said or done, not for your childhood, your first girlfriend, or anyone who hurt you.

You can seek justice for past injustices, create art about your experiences, or make meaning of your past through service, your profession, or other outlets. Those avenues are critical and important. But you cannot control what happened. So stop trying to roll back time.

You also have no control over other people.

What they think.

What they say.

What they do.

What they desire.

How they feel.

Who they listen to.

Any of it.

You can connect with them, love them, serve them, forgive them. But you can't control them.

Sure, you can use power, manipulation, or coercion to force people to do things for a season. Bosses and dictators and abusers have been using these tactics since the beginning of time. But it all comes crashing down. Anything built on control and coercion is a fragile system. And fragile systems collapse.

You can only control your thoughts and your actions. That's it.

Any impulses to "fix" your husband, or "make" your wife act a certain way, or "force" your kids to change their attitudes are futile. Any attempt to get revenge is a waste of time and energy. Because in relationships you care about, if you win and they lose, *you both lose*.

Lastly, you can't control many of the circumstances in your life.

You alone can't control the economy or housing prices or which politicians get elected or which TV shows are made. You can't control the price of gasoline or whether your mower breaks. You can't control whether your in-laws treat you like dirt or how hot it gets in Arizona in the summer. We have little or no control over other people's cancer, layoffs, or natural disasters. We have no control over famine in other parts of the world, AI's takeover of more and more jobs, or the next pandemic after the last one.

Of course, this doesn't mean we don't vote. Or that we don't donate time and money to help others. This doesn't mean we stop learning and teaching others about mental health, wellness, and nutrition. We work hard to be valuable to our company so that we don't get laid off. We work to do the right things—but we hold the outcomes loosely, with open hands.

We can only control our thoughts and our behaviors. That. Is. All. We have to let everything else go. We have to stop wishing we could control what we obviously can't.

Control what you can control.

You can control what you think. What you say. What you do. What you want. Who you speak with. Who you allow into your life and how much they influence what you believe. Where you work. Where you live. How you spend your money. How you process emotions. How you spend your time.

See how long the list is? Here's more.

You can be radically disciplined. You can be kind, regardless of the circumstances. You can do whatever it takes to laugh more and be silly and dance in the living room and have way, way more recklessly good sex with your spouse. You can exercise, eat clean, and honor your one precious body. You can do everything in your power to do maintenance, prevent where you can, and heal where you can.

Controlling your thoughts and actions is a ton of work. And it's enough.

You cannot control what happened. You control how you think about it and what you do next.

You cannot control which thoughts flash into your mind. But you control what you think of next.

Control what you can control and set the rest down.

It is a lot of heavy lifting. It is a practice. It is a discipline. It is frustrating, and you will trip and fall often. But you get back up and go again. You don't make excuses. You own your strength. You own your power.

You control your thoughts.

CHAPTER 12

Change Your Actions

In my early thirties, my knees started hurting, I had persistent pain in my neck, and my clothes were all shrinking.[107] I was falling in love with elastic, and I started buying bigger shirts and pants so I could breathe easier. I still lifted weights and I would occasionally jog, but I was certainly slowing down. My wife said I had started snoring.

One day at work, I stopped by to see one of my law professor buddies. When I walked in his office, he stepped back, looked me over in my suit and tie, and said, "Dude. You are jacked. You look like a linebacker in that suit."

He meant it as a compliment.

Except I was a former wide receiver. And a sprinter. I've always been skinny, and I hadn't suddenly loaded up with a bunch of muscles. I had just gotten fat, quietly gaining thirty-five or forty pounds over a few years.

---

107. Yeah, right . . . I wish.

I'm tall and athletic so I wore it okay . . . but the truth was on the scale. I kept telling myself this was just part of getting older. Joints are supposed to hurt as you age. Moving less is normal. Exercise is a young man's game. Squats are for high school football players. Men should get big.

I was big. Uncomfortable and big. I didn't feel good very often.

My buddy's comment inspired me to get back into action. Sort of. I began researching workout programs. Hundreds and hundreds of them. I started trying out specialized diets again. I kept looking for hacks, shortcuts, and side options. I'd try a new weight-lifting program one weekend, ditch it by Wednesday, and then start a new one the following weekend. I'd work out so hard and then be unable to move for three days. I'd recover with some fancy health bars and ice cream and then overdo it again. I was a human yo-yo.

And then one day I was talking with a friend in the health and fitness industry. I was trying to sound knowledgeable—using all the science words and insights I'd learned from the internet—while also spitting out excuse after excuse for why I wasn't exercising consistently. I wanted him to tell me the secrets of getting in shape. I wanted the perfect diet and the perfect workout.

He finally turned to me and said:

"Want to know what the best workout program is? Anything you will do consistently, every single day, for the rest of your life. That's it."

He continued. "Want to know what the perfect diet is? Quit eating processed sugar and most food in packages. Eat lots of protein and healthy fats and loads of vegetables and very, very few processed grains. Eat in moderation and don't skip the occasional ice cream with your wife or piece of birthday cake at your kid's party. Eat slow, and stop when you're full. Drink lots of water and never have soda again. Do that for the rest of your life."

And then he finished with the kicker: "Here's the secret: Do something. Anything. And do it over and over again. Every day. If you want to change your body, you have to change what you do. Quit asking me about it and start doing something."

Dude.

He was right.

And this wasn't just about my fitness. This was also about my parenting, being a good husband, being a good academic, and contributing as a community member.

If I wanted to change my life, I had to change my actions. I had to change how I lived. I had to head into the storm. I had to take control of my life, stop making excuses, and change my actions. Period.

How to Change Your Actions

The fifth and final step to developing and maintaining a well life is to change your actions for the better. Actions are the day-to-day efforts that make up your life. How you treat your body. How you treat your spiritual life. How you honor your relationships, your work, your home, your family, and your neighbors. Actions can be both big and small—from running into a burning building to save your elderly neighbor to brushing your teeth, keeping a daily gratitude journal, and not piling stacks of books around your bedside table.[108]

Our brains crave familiar. We do the same things over and over because it's predictable and our brains equate predictable with "safe." Our brains want to keep things known. Contained. In the

---

108. The number of books in stacks and piles around my bed is obnoxious. Even more ridiculous is that (a) I won't read most of them, and (b) I will order books online while sitting on my bed, next to the stacks.

well-worn rut. As I noted earlier, the brain outsources everything it can to free up space. Most of our actions are on autopilot.

This is why changing our actions is so difficult. Our brains are also always looking to solve for familiar. New husband? Your brain remembers how your dad did marriage and defaults to that story. Had an old boyfriend? Brain remembers that one too. It just replays the story with a new face or a different setting. Scratch and claw your way to losing twenty-five pounds? Our brains don't like change, which is why we can hit our magic number on the scale but then the weight seems to find its way back on.

Notice I didn't say that our brains and bodies feel good. Or healthy. Or whole.

Just safe and predictable.

When you are changing your actions, comfort can become the enemy.

Bestselling author, psychologist, and good friend Dr. Henry Cloud says, "We get comfortable with our misery, as we find ways to medicate ourselves, delude ourselves, dissociate our feelings, or get enough distance from the problem that it does not touch us directly."[109] This is why we will stay in an abusive relationship—it hurts, but it's predictable. It's the devil we know. This is why we scream and yell and choose to stay angry. Those are the stories we know.

In order to make changes, then, we have to rattle the cage. We have to take drastic action.

In this chapter we will walk through how to change your actions. Most of you will not like this chapter. I'm okay with you not liking me— just know I'm telling you the truth.

I'm going to tell you the truth not because of personal or political

---

109. Dr. Henry Cloud, *Necessary Endings: The Employees, Businesses, and Relationships That All of Us Have To Give Up*, (New York: Harper Business, 2011), 151.

agendas. I'm going to tell you the truth because I care about you and I want you to live a well and whole life.

And I know you want that too.

Stop Making Excuses

I've been a teacher and professor involved in the messiness of people's lives for several decades. I've been a researcher, crisis responder, dean of students, and a parent. I've been a basketball and track coach and a personal coach and counselor.

I've seen and heard all of your excuses.

I've even made many of those excuses myself.

Excuses like:

- I'm not really an exercise person.
- I'm an indoor guy, not an outdoor guy.
- It's too hot. They're too cold.
- You don't understand what I've been through.
- I don't really read.
- She eats poorly so I'm just stuck eating this way too.
- I just can't stop taking this personally.
- I have to take care of them because they need me.
- I *have* to let him move back in.

And millions more.

Let's just assume that some of these are true.

You've been hurt. You do feel stuck. You feel completely alone in a crowded home. It *is* hot.

And now what?

Your life is ticking, ticking, ticking away.

The only thing that matters is what you do next.

And you can't do anything if you wrap yourself up in excuses.

Go to any marathon in the United States and there will be large bodies, small bodies, and bodies with prosthetic legs. Running 26.2 miles.

I spent time working with young people at a camp in the mountains of New Mexico. One of the young men there was a gang member who was intermittently homeless and struggling with addiction. Throughout the week, he had time to be away from the chaos of home. He was able to sleep. And laugh. And think. He ran with kids his own age and had age-appropriate fun. He had an encounter with God and people who genuinely cared about him. At the end of the week, he came to me and handed me his colors (his bandana). He said he was done banging and that he was out.

I told him this was a major move—I knew it would cost him physically and psychologically. I told him I was scared for him.

He replied simply, "I know. But it's time."

You're not too old, too trapped, too poor, too rich, too high up the professional ladder, or too mired in the mud of poverty.

The first step in changing your actions is to stop making excuses for why you can't—and won't—take action.

And let's be clear: you are always taking action.

You're always doing something—something that moves you closer to the person you want to be, or something that moves you away from the person you want to be.

You are taking action all day, every day. Not taking action *is an action*. Doing nothing *is an action*.

Laying on the couch playing video games while your wife is doing bedtime with the kids is an action. Mindlessly scrolling on your phone while your husband is finishing up the yard after working a full day on the line is an action. Not exercising is an action. Choosing rage, not going to counseling, not taking your medication, not saying you're sorry, not going back to school, not cutting up your credit cards, not listening to a different point of view . . .

They are all actions.

And they are all taking you farther and farther from where you want to be. From who you want to be. From being well.

Hear me on this: I'm not blaming you for yesterday. I'm challenging you today.

Former Navy Seal and bestselling author Jocko Willink says changing your actions starts with discipline, so make the decision. He says

> Commit.
>
> Become the discipline—embrace its cold, relentless power.
>
> It will make you better and stronger and smarter and faster and healthier than anything else.
>
> Most important: it will make you free.[110]

If you want to be well, whole, and connected, you start by not making excuses.

If you want a life free of anxiety, depression, disconnection, and rage, you have to stop making excuses.

Discipline is the antidote to excuses. Discipline is just a decision, made over and over again. In the face of discipline, excuses don't matter. Because you're going to get fit anyway. You're going to work three extra jobs and pay off your credit cards and your mortgage anyway. You're going to go back to school, commit to healing from trauma, or go meet with a doctor and begin taking your depression medications anyway.

---

110. Jocko Willink, *Discipline Equals Freedom: Field Manual,* (New York: St. Marten's Press, 2020), 7.

Despite the objections, the challenges, or the excuses.
Stop making excuses.

Inventory Your Actions

The second piece to changing your actions is to take an inventory of what you're currently doing. Look at your life. It sounds intuitive, but most of us blow right past this. We get all amped up and manic to change our lives and crush our goals, but we don't know where we're starting from. We're a ball of energy bouncing from one thing to the next.

You can't run a race unless you know where the starting line is. And you can't run a race if you don't know where you're going.

Take out your journal and answer these questions:

- How do you treat your body? Are you happy with it? Does it serve you well? Do you take care of it? When's the last time you went to the doctor or the dentist? When's the last time you worked out? Do you sleep? When do you wake up? and go to bed?

- How do you treat your friends, family, and community? Do you make time for friends? Do you serve your community? Are you connected to a faith community? Do you honor your spouse? Do you make intentional time for connecting with your kids? Do you call your mom or dad? When? How often?

- How do you treat your work? Are you fulfilled in your professional role? Do you make enough money? Are you contributing to something bigger than yourself? Is your work environment healthy? Do you work hard? Are you contributing to a major mission or purpose? Do you look to lead and grow?

- How do you treat your faith community? Are you in a season of doubt? Have you given up on faith altogether? Do you regularly practice prayer, meditation, reading Scripture, and meeting with a group of believers? Do you worship with fellow believers?

- How do you treat your home environment? Is your home a wreck? A cluttered mess? Are you obsessive about cleanliness and order? Do you honor your possessions? Do you know where things are?

- How do you treat others? Do the people in your life treat you with dignity, respect, and care? Do you drive the speed limit? Get impatient and aggressive with restaurant staff and customer service representatives? Do you owe other people money—and if so, how much and to whom? Do you hurt or abuse others? Do you need to get out of any abusive relationships?

Don't overthink these. Just write down the first few things that come to mind. Be honest.

Take an inventory of your daily actions. Your everyday actions make up who you are. Your actions make up your identity.

Now I'll ask you: What is your perceived identity? Who are you?

Pay close attention here. I ordered the questions this way on purpose.

I didn't ask you about your identity first and then your actions second. I asked how you live your life. Not your fantasy about how great you are. And not your skewed image of how crappy you're doing. I asked about your daily actions. Your habits. How you live your life.

Your identity is the sum total of your actions.

Many of you are not doing nearly as well as you think. And many of you are not doing nearly as poorly as you think. Some of you are pretty honest with yourself.

When you're well, your actions line up with your perceived identity. You're living up to the picture in your head. For most people who aren't living well lives, their actions and who they want to be do not line up. They want to be thinner but they eat trash. They want to save money and get out of debt but they won't make a budget. They want to be a better spouse but they haven't sat down with their wife or husband to define what "better" even means.

Our actions define our identities. The sum total of our actions tells us who we are. But when it comes to changing your actions—really making life-change and building new habits—there's a fascinating plot twist.

Life-change starts not with racing out to do a bunch of new actions. Changing your actions begins with reverse-engineering the action/identity equation. It begins with a change in identity.

The obvious question is: How do I change my identity?

Change Your Identity

This is the moment where a lot of people go off track. Almost everybody wants more peace, to be more kind, and to sleep better. We are a culture obsessed with goals! We're focused on the number of wins or the specific behaviors. We make a list of (somewhat arbitrary) goals—some specific and some unwieldy and vague. We declare well-meaning proclamations that inspire no long-term behavior change and all but assure failure—because there is no change in identity.

Big goals are fine. In fact, they're great. But chasing wins or goals can quickly derail you. I'm a lifelong Houston Astros fan. I've seen what happens when a group becomes obsessed with chasing wins.

Goal-chasing sprints are short-lived because you're not going anywhere or becoming anything. You just want to make little tweaks on the edges. You're just changing up a few things.

- "I need to eat better."
- "I want to get more rest."
- "I need to be a more helpful son."
- "I want to fit into that dress."
- "I want to be hotter and have whiter teeth."
- "I'm not happy in my job. Maybe I should get another one."

We get caught up in half-baked, half-hearted, wet-toast attempts at trying to stop doing this or start doing that. Or we scratch out a few hard-knock goals and white-knuckle our way across the finish line.

These approaches never work for long.

Why? Because wherever you go,

There you are.

No matter where you end up, you go with you.

As international bestselling author and habit expert James Clear says, when we start focusing on what we want to change or accomplish, we can get there . . . but if we don't make internal changes, we are no different on arrival.[111]

Sure, I can grit my teeth toward some weight loss, but I'm still the same guy who gained the weight in the first place. Sure, I can force myself to prioritize sleep for a few weeks, but if I haven't done the hard work of changing who I am and the habits I live by, my changes won't stick. Sure, I can vow to never yell at my kids again. But I still haven't dealt with my anger, my frustration, or my marriage.

---

111. James Clear, *Atomic Habits: An Easy & Proven Way to Build Good Habits & Break Bad Ones*, (New York: Avery, 2018), 55.

Same with new jobs, new cars, pay raises, and new grills, guns, and guitars. They are cool for a bit—sometimes really cool—but you are still the same. You'll be on to the next new thing soon enough.

To change your actions, you have to decide who you are and who you want to become. You have to *create new identities*. What does this look like in practice?

Clear says that people should not "begin the process of changing their habits by focusing on what they want to achieve . . . , [instead] we start by focusing on *who we wish to become*."[112] He further suggests that "what you do is an indication of the type of person you believe that you are—either consciously or unconsciously."[113]

So instead of saying that you want to lose some weight, you have to first decide to be a person who is an excellent steward of their one precious body. You are a person who takes care of themselves so that you can think clearly, run around with the kids, have incredible, spontaneous sex, work a second job to pay off debt, and have the energy to serve your church and your community. You honor your body through movement, rest, good food, and good mental, relational, and spiritual inputs. And by honoring your body, you honor every single person you come into contact with.

Instead of saying you're a mom and wife who needs to quit yelling, you have to first decide you're a woman who honors and loves herself. And you're a woman who treats her family with dignity and respect. You're a woman who does not traumatize her children. You're a person who does not yell. Ever.

See how this works? Our actions make up our identity. And to make lasting behavioral change, you start from who you wish to become and work in reverse.

---

112. Clear, *Atomic Habits,* 31. Emphasis mine.
113. Clear, *Atomic Habits,* 34.

You start changing your actions by first changing your identity.

When you decide that you are a woman who will always treat her children with dignity and respect, even when they make bone-headed choices, you stop yelling as a default. When you choose to be a person who honors their body, you make better diet and exercise choices on the way to a healthier life. You will lose weight on the way to wherever it is you're going.

Clear says, "The more deeply a thought or action is tied to your identity, the more difficult it is to change it."[114] So after you decide who you're going to be, you must then "prove it to yourself with small wins."[115] Or as the Avett Brothers sing, "Decide who to be and go be it." Which leads us to the next step.

Determine the Actions toward Your New Identities

The next step in changing your actions is all about the little wins. Little wins are the actions you'll take to create your new identity. These are the painfully clear, detailed moves that will nudge you toward who you want to become. You can't lose a hundred pounds in a weekend (without some complicated surgery). You lose a hundred pounds one meal at a time. One workout at a time. One thought and one choice at a time.

For example:

Old Perceived Identity: I love, honor, and respect everyone. I'm a good guy, a good leader, and a good example in my home and my workplace.

---

114. Clear, *Atomic Habits*, 35.
115. Clear, *Atomic Habits*, 39.

Action Inventory: I see that I am always late. To meetings, parties, and lunches with mentors. Three minutes, fifteen minutes, or forty-five minutes—I am always late. I have a clock in my bedroom, and I try to pay attention to it, but I'm not obsessive or anything. I usually try to cram too much into my mornings or in between meetings. I don't wear a watch and I don't consistently check my online calendar. My actions do not correlate with someone who honors and respects everyone.

New Identity: I am a person who deeply respects and honors other people.

Detailed Actions:

1. Since I am a person who deeply respects and honors other people, as far as it depends on me,[116] I will never, ever be late. I will always be on time so as to be a good steward of others' time.
    a. This means that at 10:00 a.m. tomorrow, I will go to a store and buy a watch, a lunch bag, a planner, and an actual alarm clock. I will be home by noon, and I will sit at my kitchen table and fill out my planner, set and put on my watch, and set my alarm clock.
    b. This means my planner must be clean, simple, and accurate.
    c. This means I need to make my lunch and decide my daily routine the night before.

---

116. Sometimes there is a car wreck on the way to work. Sometimes you or your child is sick. Sometimes life happens.

    d. This means I need to iron and lay out my clothes the night before.

    e. This means I need to ignore any social media until after my first work meeting.

This means I will also set up an accountability program where I donate $10 to my friend's favorite charity every time I am late anywhere.

I do these things because I am a guy who deeply respects and honors other people.

See? You start with the identity, and then you get specific about the actions. About your little wins.

Here's another example.

Old Perceived Identity: You want to help other people live well and whole lives.

Action Inventory: I'm always reading blogs, watching various news sources, and consuming as much information as possible. I want to always be ready to give people answers to their most vexing challenges. Yet I don't take time for myself because I'm all about helping others. Sleep is for lazy people, nutrition science is nonsense, I don't have time for friends, and exercise is for meatheads. Those are my attitudes way deep down inside. Over time, I've become more and more anxious and stressed. I've noticed that when I give people answers, they seem a bit distraught afterward. I wind people up and make them more stressed. Even though I'm trying to help by giving them information, I'm passing on my anxious presence to them.

New Identity: I am a non-anxious person who is a peaceful presence for those who come into contact with me.

Detailed Actions:

1. Since I am a non-anxious person who spreads peace, I need to work on my anxiety alarms. I also must learn how to be a peaceful presence.

   a. This means I will call a counselor tomorrow at 8:30 a.m. and make an appointment to deal with my childhood trauma and my deployment-related PTSD. I will make changes in my budget until I can afford to keep attending these important sessions. I may have to cancel my streaming accounts and not go out to eat for a few months.

   b. This means I will make an appointment with a local doctor to get some lab work done to make sure my anxiety is not really just my exhausted, stressed, over-caffeinated, or inflamed body.

   c. This means I will begin every day with meditation, prayer, journaling, and gratitude.

   d. This means I will exercise every morning at 5:01 a.m.

   e. This means I will cut out grains and sugar, limit my caffeine intake to tea instead of coffee, and I will take a lot of fish oil and Vitamin D/K for a season.[117]

---

117. This should go without saying, but check with your doctor before you start taking supplements or medications. AND the research on fish oil's effect on certain mental health challenges is extraordinary. I take 2–3 grams of high-quality fish oil every single day. I also give it to my kids.

    f. This means I will clean and organize my life so that it is not cluttered with junk, chaos, and disorganization.

    g. This means I will make an appointment to share a meal or tea with a good friend or friends at least once a week.

    h. With my remaining time, I will commit to following credible, non-bonkers information sources and utilizing real experts who are working and researching in the fields I care about. I will turn off the news and limit mindless media consumption.

Develop your identity, and then work backwards toward the little wins. Be demanding and relentless. When it comes to each new identity, be very specific. Be very clear. Be directive. And with your action steps, be even more clear, including dates, times, and durations.[118]

Include Others

Lebron James has a nutritionist, a head coach, former coaches, mentors, a personal trainer, a massage therapist, business partners, and teammates.

Mike Tyson had Cus D'Amato and other trainers.

George St. Pierre had Firas Zahabi, the team at Jackson-Wink, a nutritionist, and other wrestling, gymnastic, and strength partners and coaches.

Dave Ramsey has his Eagles Group, his Operating Board, his close-knit family, and his close personal friends.

I have my Three Pines guys, Craig and Trevor, Buddy and Tucker, Mike and Tom, Todd and Jon, Jennifer and Melissa, Kevin and

---

118. Clear, *Atomic Habits*, 70–71.

Michael, Randal and Josh, Randy and Slade, Steve and JP, my wife, and a number of professors and colleagues. I have also had multiple therapists. Coaches. Trainers. Professors.

King Arthur had his knights of the round table.

Bruce Springsteen has the E Street Band.

Johnny had his Cobra Kai crew.

Jesus had his disciples.

I've said it throughout this book and I'll say it again: You can't be well by yourself. You need community. You need people to help you and encourage you and support you and cheer you on. You also need people to tell you the truth and pick you up when you've fallen off the wagon. Community and accountability is critical. Connection is a powerful tool to help you keep focused and keep moving forward.

And hopefully you see how this all works together. Remember back to chapter 10, when we discussed how to connect and make friends?

- If you want to exercise three times a week, find two other people to join you at the gym. Or join a running group. Or start one. Get connected as you get moving. Or sign up with a CrossFit gym or for a Brazilian ju-jitsu class.
- If you need to work through some serious trauma from your childhood, make an appointment with a specialist. Yeah, it costs money—but so does rehab, divorce court, buying bulk snacks at the local warehouse club, and all our other adaptive coping strategies. Chances are you'll have better success with healing and focused recovery when you're connected to a professional or a team of professionals. Go to group. Work on your addictions in a recovery community. Practice relationships with your therapist. Take your medications.

- If you want to learn to pray more, pray differently, and pray more meaningfully, start attending a small group or a prayer group. Join a Bible study or a service community. Take a course at a local college. Find people you can rely on and learn from.

Changing your actions often puts you in direct relationship with others who have similar interests or goals.

And yes, getting connected is an action. It is something you choose to do.

Paying attention to your thoughts, especially those that no longer serve you, is also an action. When you intentionally choose to change your thoughts, you are taking action.

Each of the practices informs the others, so use that to your advantage.

Are you beginning to see how it all works together?

Evaluate Your Actions

The last piece to changing your actions is to evaluate what you're doing. Are your actions getting you closer to the person you want to become? Toward your new identities?

Evaluating your actions is similar to taking inventory, except you are doing it live and in real time. You look at your actions throughout your day and across a few months. You see the world with a curious and honest eye, always asking if you're on the right track. How do you know? Are you keeping a training log? A reading log? A course list? A journal?

This doesn't have to be complicated. In fact, it's really asking yourself a simple question: *Is this working?* Do I know why this is working? Can I repeat these findings? Do my friends and community agree it's working?

As you establish your new identities, and you construct new routines, habits, and actions, make it a regular part of your life to evaluate how you're doing. As you move through the process of stopping some things and starting new things, pay attention to how you respond physically, emotionally, spiritually, and relationally. Check for old bricks finding their way back into your backpack. Always check for new bricks. Remember to be curious when you fall off the wagon and not judgmental. You're learning something new.

You decided you want to be a person who takes care of their body, and you've spent the past ninety days changing your diet and getting more sleep. You also joined a running group so you'd have accountability.

Is it working? Are you taking better care of your body? Are you closer to wellness than you were ninety days ago? How do you know? How do you feel? Are you tracking the appropriate data points? Read back over your gratitude journal and your calendar and look for patterns.

You were born into a legacy of abuse. You were abused as a child, and your brain has been doing its best for the past twenty years to avoid future trauma by hiding from relationships. But now you're facing it head-on. You're doing the hard work. You've been seeing a trauma counselor for six months. You're doing EMDR and body work. Faithfully. You've been vulnerable and honest. You have a small group of friends, a trustworthy faith community, and a dedicated yoga practice.

Are these new practices working? Are you able to think about those traumatic moments from the past without your body spinning out on you? Does your body feel safe? Are you willing to forgive and set the bricks down?

If the answer is yes, outstanding. Keep taking little steps. Over and over and over. Keep healing. Keep improving.

If the answer is no—if what you're doing isn't working—that's okay too. In fact, *it's great*. You got new data. You explored uncharted territory. You were brave and took a swing at the dragon. If that action hasn't brought you closer to wellness and wholeness and peace, at least you've learned something new about yourself.

When your attempts to change your actions aren't working, you have two choices:

1. Keep going a little longer to see if the results improve. In this case, it's best if you give yourself a specific timeframe. "I'm going to try this for six more weeks," or something like that.
2. Talk over your situation with a friend, professional, and mentor, and if everyone agrees, drop what you're doing and try something new.

Reflect on your actions and make the adjustments you need to continue making progress.

The Return of the Excuses

You can expect your excuses to reemerge. It happens to the toughest and strongest of us. You'll be cruising along in your new identities—in two days, two months, or two years—and *WHAM!* You'll be tired of eating healthy. You'll be exhausted by being so conscious of your thoughts all the time. You'll get laid off and instantly come up with four excuses for not getting another job. Bestselling author Steven Pressfield calls it "The Resistance."[119] It's normal.

And it's death.

As I've said several times, our culture has become one of complaining, whining, and indecision. A culture of excuse makers. We overthink too much. We Google problems for hours and days. We talk about what we might do or not do with every person who will listen. We watch hundreds of videos or listen to numerous podcasts trying to "hack" our way into a better version of our lackluster life. Every website has product reviews, opinions, or other ways to validate procrastination. We keep gathering data as an antidote to anxiety, but we don't put the data to work.

Eric Thomas says, "If you have to talk to more than three people about the same problem, you don't want help, you want attention."[120]

Ouch.

So stop talking and do something.

When the excuses show back up, acknowledge them—and then go do what must be done. Do it anyway.

Start something. Or STOP something. Quit something. Begin something.

Go see a counselor. Go see a medical doctor. Change your diet. Call a friend and invite them over. Be the only one. Get up earlier. Run. Walk. Stretch. Meditate. Write your thoughts down. Examine them for evidence. Sleep and rest for once.

Just. Do. Something.

Stop yelling at your kid. Set up boundaries with your parents. Pay off your soul-sucking debts and be free. Choose happier

---

119. Steven Pressfield, *The War of Art: Break Through the Blocks and Win Your Inner Creative Battles,* (New York: Black Irish Entertainment LLC, 2002), 7.
120. Social media post.

thoughts. Read books, especially fiction. Fix something. Build something. Set some goals and start working toward them.

Just. Do. Something.

You have so much more power than you think you do. You have so much more grit and capacity than you think you do.

You don't have enough time? Sell your television and leave your smartphone in a drawer.

You've got time.

Not enough money? Get a third and fourth job and sell everything else along with your TV, including your car. Go back to school. Don't go inside a restaurant unless you work there. Get a roommate. Pack up and move to middle America.

Can't get out of debt? Join a Financial Peace University class and get to work. Make a budget. Live on less than you make. Stop complaining and be relentless.

Can't lose weight? Consult with a doctor, trainer, nutritionist, or a mental health practitioner—or all four. Pick an exercise program, any proven program, and get to work. Get online and find a healthy nutrition plan and follow it every single day. Improve your health each day.

Can't play the guitar? Take free lessons on the internet. Find people to play with.

Want to speak Spanish? Rosetta Stone. Or more free lessons on the internet. Find someone to converse with to help you practice.

The time has come when you need to act, decisively and intentionally. You've made your list of small wins. Now get to it.

Anne Lamott says you cannot "will this to happen. It is a matter of persistence and faith and hard work. So you might as well just *go ahead and get started.*"[121]

---

121. Anne Lamott, *Bird by Bird: Some Instructions on Writing and Life,* (New York: Anchor Books, 1994), 7. Emphasis mine.

Nassim N. Taleb has observed that "a single person with courage can bring down a collective composed of wimps."[122]

Jocko Willink summarizes, "Everyone wants some magic pill—some life hack—that eliminates the need to do the work. But that does not exist. No. You have to do the work. You've got to hold the line. You've got to MAKE IT HAPPEN. So. Dig in. Find the Discipline. Be the Discipline. That's it."[123]

Dr. Nadine Burke Harris says, "I think folks out there are waiting for a fancy pill to show up and they're missing the point that we, as humans, have a profound power to heal ourselves and one another."[124]

And I could go on and on.

My point here is this: Change your actions. Begin doing something. And if you've been doing something and it's not working, do something else *different*, something else *new*.

Just keep going.

The Tortoise Always Wins

My good friend Dave Ramsey says he reads the fable *The Tortoise and the Hare* every single year. And every time he reads it, the tortoise always wins.

The tortoise isn't flashy, sexy, or even more skilled. But the tortoise just keeps going.

And he wins every single time.

Just like you.

Little steps, taken over and over, for the rest of your life.

---

122. Nassim Nicholas Taleb, *Antifragile: Things That Gain from Disorder*, (New York: Random House, 2012), 420.

123. Willink, *Discipline Equals Freedom*, 69. Capitalization in the original.

124. Harris, *The Deepest Well*, 169.

It's hard at first. And it usually gets easier.

But other things come up. You have a new kid. There's a recession. You blow out your knee. Your wife leaves. You're in the middle of a special diet and your husband brings home pizza. You get fired. Your boyfriend cheats on you again.

And you start all over again. With the stories, the community, the thoughts, and the actions.

You're not going to lose sixty-five pounds tomorrow. You're not going to heal from childhood trauma in a month. You're not going to heal your marriage in a single weekend retreat. You're not going to finish your master's degree in a semester.

Changing your actions is a daily decision, for the rest of your life.

But you can take the first step. And then the next. And then the next.

You'll fall down. Your friends will help you up. Sometimes you'll be alone and you'll pull yourself up. And you'll keep going. You'll keep writing down the stories and thoughts and you'll keep demanding evidence. You'll refine and transform your identities, and you'll keep changing your actions, one at a time.

Here's my advice: go slow and give yourself some grace.

If you put in the work, things *will* change. The light of hope will grow brighter and brighter.

You'll wake up one day and realize you feel lighter inside. Some of the darkness or pressure is gone. You'll skip the morning coffee because you don't need it.[125]

You'll own your doubts and walk back into a local church building. You'll seek to rediscover.

Or you'll go out for a jog and suddenly realize, *This feels good.* Someone will cut you off in traffic and you'll say a quiet prayer for

---

125. I mean . . . I don't want to get carried away here.

him instead of flipping him off. Someone will accidentally ding your door in a store parking lot and your first response will be to laugh. You'll choose sex over Netflix. You'll say I'm sorry instead of calling your ex.

This is peace.

Awful things will still happen. People will pass away; strangers will drink and drive. Your mother-in-law will still throw fits like a child. You'll slip into old patterns now and again. You'll occasionally make some bad choices. Politicians will keep lying. You'll compromise your values and your partner's values. Other things will go down that are way outside your control.

And you'll still have peace. Kindness. Self-control. Joy. Love. Patience.

You'll get back up and choose discipline. You'll choose action. And you'll go again.

You'll be tethered to people who care about you. You'll have much better control over what you think and how your thoughts drive you each day. And you'll understand how to make both little and big changes in your actions and routines when necessary.

You'll have a different life.

You'll be well. Whole.

You'll be free.

CHAPTER 13

Redemption

One night I was teaching a graduate school course and my phone started ringing.

This was a major no-no, only because I always made such a big deal about how I hated when students were on their cell phones in class.

And so you can imagine my surprise when my own phone started ringing right in the middle of my lecture. Almost in unison, my students all went "Ooooooooohhhh ... busted, Dr. D!" "You have to leave class and try again next week!" "No phones allowed, Doc!"

Their ribbing was well deserved. I was embarrassed and making fun of myself too. We all had a good laugh.

I was wearing a suit and I started doing the pocket-pat dance, trying to locate exactly where my phone was. I found it and caught a quick glance of who it was before I turned it off.

When I saw the name on the caller ID, my heart sank.

I knew this name ... and I knew what this name meant.

I signaled to my class that I would be right back and I stepped into the hallway to take the call.

"Good evening, this is John Delony."

"Hey Dr. Delony," a frightened voice said on the other line. "This is Eric Turner, Tom Turner's father."[126]

"Hi, Eric. Call me John. What's going on?"

"Well . . . (pause) . . . I received some troubling messages from Tom, and several of his friends reached out to me and my wife, letting us know that they haven't heard from him in several days. The last time I heard from Tom was yesterday."

My heart sank further. Tom was one of my favorite students of all time: funny, brilliant, introspective, and compassionate. He also suffered from major depression and had spent several years wrestling with dark thoughts and attempted suicide. So when Tom's father reached out to tell me that Tom had sent troubling notes to his friends and loved ones and that he was missing, I knew it was serious.

I immediately dismissed my class, called campus police, and sprinted across campus to the graduate school apartments. I ran as fast as I could in my dress shoes and suit, and I met the police officers at Tom's residence hall. The student worker got permission to let us in Tom's room. He wasn't there.

Campus police partnered with the local city police and Tom's cell phone carrier, and he was ultimately located a few states over, next to a campground where the Turner family camped when he was a kid. His phone was turned off, but for Mr. Turner and the rest of the Turner family, at least local authorities had a general geographic location to check the following day.

Later in the evening, I told Mr. Turner to give me a call during the night if there was any new news. We agreed to check back in with each other the following morning.

---

126. I've changed the names in this story to protect the family's privacy.

The next morning I went to my office. As I always did when I was worried about a student, I was holding out hope for the best while also holding a sliver of space for worst-case news.

Sometime midmorning, the silence in my office was interrupted by my cell phone ringing. I grabbed the phone and saw that it was Mr. Turner. I whispered a quick prayer, took a deep breath, and answered the phone. I was not expecting what I heard.

Mr. Turner was overjoyed.

"We found him, Dr. Delony! We found him!"

"What?" I exclaimed. "That's FANTASTIC! Where? When?"

My shoulders dropped. I realized I had not taken a breath in hours. I exhaled deeply.

Mr. Turner told me he had not yet talked to Tom, but that the cell phone company had just called and notified him that Tom's cell phone had been turned on and that they had identified a direct location. Authorities had been notified and were on their way. Just as I cheered again with Mr. Turner, my office phone started ringing.

I interrupted the happy father and told him to hang on one quick second while I answered my office phone. I was grinning ear to ear. I had my cell phone wedged between my head and my shoulder as I grabbed my office phone. I quickly untangled the cord, pulled the phone up to my other ear, and said, "Hi, this is John Delony's office. What's up?"

The stoic voice on the other end of the phone was quiet yet resolute.

"Good morning, Mr. Delony. My name is Sergeant Fox of the State Police Department. I was given your number by our detective who was investigating your missing student."

"Yes, sir. Thanks for calling. I'm on the phone with his dad and I heard that he's been located?"

"Yes, Mr. Delony. I regret to inform you that we have located your student, Tom Turner, and he died by suicide. The officer on the scene found him and turned on his cell phone to assist with identification."

Razor-sharp inhale. I could not breathe.

On one ear I held my cell phone, talking to an ecstatic father who believed he'd found his missing son. On the other ear I held my office phone, talking to a state trooper who had the tragic responsibility of calling me and letting me know that my student was no longer alive.

Tom was dead.

And there I stood, with a phone on each ear, stuck in a gritty, twisted space somewhere between hope and truth. The hope of a father who loved his son very, very much—and the truth that a brilliant young man died way, way too soon.

In the years following that tragic, gut-wrenching day, I have repeatedly found myself, my family, my community, and beyond, in that same place.

We are all standing somewhere between hope and truth.

Stuck Between Hope and Truth

What we're doing isn't working.

We've added hundreds of thousands of mental health workers and the dams are still overflowing.

We've written millions of psychotropic medication prescriptions and addictions are up, drug abuse is up, and mental health challenges are skyrocketing.

We've created manual after manual of diagnostics to label, distill, and judge people who are struggling with loneliness and dysfunctional relationships, systemic injustice, a lack of safety, and trauma.

We've outsourced the fundamentals of life: our bodies, our

food, our time, our relationships, our God, our full range of human emotions, and our end of life to companies and technology, hacks and quacks, and endless pills and medications.

We are clinging to hope that these things will save us. The truth is they aren't. They won't. They can't.

We're stuck here between hope and truth.

We hope that just the right workout program, just the right medication, just the right girlfriend, just the right marriage seminar, just the right app on our phones, or just the right parenting book will show up and the lightbulbs will all turn on, and we'll be okay.

We hope that we can hate and shame ourselves into better bodies, marriages, or sex lives.

We hope we can endlessly and ceaselessly medicate our kids with no consequences. We hope we can continue to eat trash and never move our bodies and still feel good.

We hope we can scroll and scroll and scroll ourselves to better lives. Or we can binge away our sadness.

Thumbs-downing and scrolling is the new fight-or-flight. We hope we can engage in these insane mini-wars all day every day and not come away with any scars.

But your heart knows the truth, physiologically and spiritually. Your body knows too.

The truth is, the ride is coming to an end.

Like driving a car without changing your oil—at some point, the car is going to stop. You can stop at an oil-change place and get the work done, or your car will stop on you. Or like my friend Melissa's car, the engine will melt on the side of the road, never to run again.

The answer is to own your stories, acknowledge your reality, get connected, change your thoughts, and change your actions. And everything is different.

It will hurt. It will ache. It will feel like too much a lot of the time. There will be blood and scabs and scars and learning how to walk again and being okay with not being as fast as you once were.

This. Will. Be. Hard.

But you're worth getting well, being treated well, and living a joyful, free, and adventure-filled life.

You are worth it.

Put the Bricks Down

One afternoon during my first few months of co-hosting the radio show, I received a phone call from a woman who lived in Alaska.

She told me all she ever wanted in her life was to be a stay-at-home mom. She wanted to build a home for her family, have a loving partnership with her husband, and pour herself into her children. This was her dream.

Unfortunately, in the middle of her dream she learned her husband had racked up somewhere close to $750,000 in business debt under his name. This meant that he and his wife had to pay it off as consumer debt. Imagine being $750,000 in debt. Her family was in big, big trouble.

To their credit, this woman and her husband got to work. She took a job, he took several, and they started plowing through the debt. Year after year. Dollar by dollar. I was blown away by their work ethic, integrity, and grind. Her husband had swung for the fences and missed, and now everyone was pitching in to pick up the pieces.

When this woman called my show, she and her husband had almost paid off every single debt. They had less than a hundred thousand dollars left to pay back. They had almost pulled this thing off.

But her last child was about to leave for college. Which meant her dream of being a stay-at-home mother was over. She missed it. She looked up and realized she'd been working for more than fifteen years, forced into a life she didn't choose or want. And now the life she'd always longed for was walking out the door. It was gone. Her dream was over.

She said to me on the phone, "All I ever wanted was to be a stay-at-home mom, and my husband screwed up and took that from me. I'm just so angry with him, and I don't think I'll ever be able to forgive him."

Wow.

I could hear her hurt. She was talking to me from three thousand miles away, but I could hear the anguish in her voice. The loss. The rage. She had stood by her man in spite of his mistakes, and it had cost her everything. I felt angry on her behalf just thinking about it.

But here she was. There was no way to recapture the past. She had to own her past and then decide what came next.

I said, "Ma'am, with all due respect, you've got to put that down."

Silence.

I continued, "From this point forward, every minute you choose being resentful, angry, or bitter, is a minute you're choosing to have less joy, less love, and less fun. When you choose anger and resentment, you're choosing to not fully live whatever life you have left. To be whole, you have to set down your anger, forgive your husband, and let those things go."

About a month later, I received a handwritten letter from the woman. Not just a letter, either. She had included a series of miniature quilts with crocheted words across them. The words were: *Anger. Resentment. Bitterness.* They were beautiful. I could tell she'd put a lot of energy and work into them. In the letter, she said she'd spent a lot of time making those miniature quilts—cutting, sewing, stitching—and in the process, she literally felt her anger and resentment leave her body. She felt her body release.

She wrote me, "I've got peace. I let them go, and I'm done with them."

She set them down. She chose new thoughts, and she chose new actions. And her heart changed. She wanted to change her heart, so she got to work.

Now it's your turn.

You can't change the old sentences. They have a period at the end. But you can write something new. Something you've never written before.

We're all waiting to see what you'll write next.

Redeem the Bricks

And so you've stood up.

Look around. Your bricks are out of your backpack, and they're scattered all over your house and yard. You've been checking them for evidence. You've spent time healing your body's response to old traumas. To the abuse. The tragic and sudden loss. To the hatred. To the racism and sexism. To the disgust. To the physical pain. To the dark nights of your theological soul.

You are making friends and re-imagining and re-creating your friendships, your workplace, and your marriage.

You are changing your thoughts and your actions. You are leaning into addiction reduction. You are setting boundaries and practicing at holding them firm.

Your backpack is lighter now. You're meditating. You've made peace with old religious wounds and you've knocked on the door of a new church. You're seeing a counselor, and you and your romantic partner are in couples' counseling. You're taking care of your body. Your mind. You've got a morning routine, and you're telling the truth. You're working out regularly.

You have an answer for the one terrifying question: *What do you want out of your one, tiny, wild life?*

But you also can't help but look around and wonder, *What do I do with all these bricks?*

You redeem them.

Whether you knew it or not, these bricks can be redeemed. Your life and hurt and pain will not be wasted.

Your bricks can become a new part of the great old brick road. A road that is thousands of years in the making, formed from the challenges, trails, and triumphs of millions of people who have come before you. Those people were brave, strong, worthy, and enough.

Just like you.

Your bricks will become an essential part of this road. Pavers on the path.

This is legacy.

And this is the road your kids will walk on. The road your neighbors and your community and your grandkids and friends will walk on. This is the road future generations will take to get to work, to visit loved ones, to go to school, and to make their journey back home. This is the road people will head back to when they get lost.

Because as bestselling author and songwriter Andrew Peterson says, "We all get lost sometimes."

Their life will be better because *you* did the work. Because you said, "No more."

The road is peace and deep breaths. It is kindness and patience and a quick smile instead of flashing anger. The road is gentleness and self-control, even when things seem or feel out of control.

The road is ownership, discipline, and responsibility.

The road is freedom.

A New Picture of Wellness

The irony is thick in the air today. I'm writing this last chapter from my front porch, under a beautiful moon, in the woods just outside of Nashville, Tennessee.

And I have Covid. And so does my wife and our two young kids.

We were cautious and we tried to be smart, but it still got us. My daughter had to miss the first two weeks of kindergarten, and my son had to miss his first (and second) cross-country meets. We've been quarantined for days now, and the kids are up and running around a bit. Our cases have been uncomfortable but not catastrophic. We've been fortunate.

This week's international news, though, in multiple places across the globe, has been deeply disturbing and devastating. Heartbreaking.

My grandfather is ninety-four years old and he is still working through later-stage cancer. A few weeks ago, my mom, who is seventy-one, was heading out to a month-long writing sabbatical in the New Mexico mountains. She randomly stumbled while putting gas in her car and broke her shoulder clean off the ball joint. I have several friends whose marriages are on life support. We've had three suicides in our community this month.

And the aftermath of the pandemic and politics and job changes and re-routed dreams and homeschooling and bitcoin and moving and everything else has been . . . exhausting. It's all been challenging for my marriage. And my kids are struggling, even though they are carrying a brave face.

Several good friends have died.

If you're like me, you can get all misty-eyed and inspired about changing your life, your relationships, and your mental health. You can even gut things out for a few weeks. But then the realities of life—the gritty, bloody-knuckled, scarred realities—finally show back up in your mirror.

You began to wonder what you're even aiming for. Why be well if there are still earthquakes and economic meltdowns and melting ice and hatred and childhood traumas?

I mean, what are we even doing?

The Picture

Wellness is an approach to life. It is an action, a way of being—not a destination.[127]

Being well and living whole are not achievements. They are not places you go or levels you accomplish. They are directions. A road map.

Wellness and wholeness are ongoing.

And unfortunately for achievers or Enneagram wizards or people who love the world wrapped in neat little diagnostics, one-size-fits-all programs, or Myers-Briggs packages, joyful living doesn't work that way.

You are unique. As am I. As are the billions of people all around the planet. To say there is one right way that "well" is supposed to look is at best naïve and at worst maleficent.

Being well and whole doesn't mean everything will always be perfect. It doesn't mean that your mom won't get cancer, that your best friend won't steal from you, or that you won't say something that deeply and profoundly hurts people who love you. It doesn't mean that you won't have hard questions about God, and it doesn't mean that there won't be war or economic catastrophes.

---

127. Emily Nagoski, PhD, Amelia Nagoski, DMA, *Burnout: The Secret to Unlocking the Stress Cycle*, (New York: Ballantine Books, 2019), 28.

Being well means that, come what may, you will have peace.

Even when the world is on fire, you will remain patient.

When you are cut off in traffic, you will retain your power and choose kindness.

When you remember those who deeply hurt you, or when you are deeply hurt in the future, you will choose forgiveness. You will choose not to carry hate and anger and bricks. You will dust off your sandals and move on.

You will be aggressive and strong on the ball fields and in business—and you will front-hug your sons, get on the floor and play eye to eye with your daughters, and eagerly sit through dreadful theater performances and recitals.

You will weep bitterly. You will grieve for months if not years. And you will still honor your body. You will spend more time with humans and less time with electronics. You will support your political party and religious denomination—but not blindly—and you will stand up and speak boldly when the time demands.

You will meet Jesus.

You will hold life loosely because it was never yours to begin with.

So I'm sitting on my porch, with Covid, under the moon, with the world on fire, and I am at peace.

Not because I'm toxically positive.

Not because I'm delusional.

Not because I'm out of touch.

Not because I'm lucky.

I am at peace because I am well. Because I'm connected to deep and extraordinary relationships. Because my backpack is lighter than it once was. Because I have a process. Because one day my time will come and I'm okay with that. I have accountability. I set obnoxious goals and I work hard to reach them. And if I miss my goals, my life doesn't end. I just start over. I also rest and love my family. And I love God—and I'm still figuring out what that means and how that looks.

I have peace for the long arc of humanity too. Things look messy and dark in the smoke, but I believe our best days are ahead of us.

I feel miserable right now but I'm smiling. You and I have so, so much work to do.

But I believe in both of us.

And I'm not going to quit. I hope you won't either.

Let's go.

FOR FURTHER READING

Antifragile: Things That Gain from Disorder by Nassim Nicholas Taleb

Baby Steps Millionaires: How Ordinary People Built Extraordinary Wealth—and How You Can Too by Dave Ramsey

Behave: The Biology of Humans at Our Best and Worst by Robert M. Sapolsky

The Body Keeps the Score: Brain, Mind, and Body in the Healing of Trauma by Bessel van der Kolk, MD

Boundaries: When to Say Yes, How to Say No to Take Control of Your Life by Henry Cloud and John Townsend

Burnout: The Secret to Unlocking the Stress Cycle by Emily Nagoski, PhD, and Amelia Nagoski, DMA

Come as You Are: The Surprising New Science That Will Transform Your Sex Life by Emily Nagoski, PhD

The Deepest Well: Healing the Long-Term Effects of Childhood Trauma and Adversity by Nadine Burke Harris, MD

The Denial of Death by Ernest Becker

Discipline Equals Freedom by Jocko Willink

Dopamine Nation: Finding Balance in the Age of Indulgence by Anna Lembke, MD

Finding Meaning: The Sixth Stage of Grief by David Kessler

Food Fix: How to Save Our Health, Our Economy, Our Communities, and Our Planet—One Bite at a Time by Mark Hyman, MD

Hooked: Food, Free Will, and How the Food Giants Exploit Our Addictions by Michael Moss

How Can I Get Through to You? Closing the Intimacy Gap Between Men and Women by Terrence Real

I Don't Want to Talk About It: Overcoming the Secret Legacy of Male Depression by Terrence Real

The Ideal Team Player: How to Recognize and Cultivate the Three Essential Virtues by Patrick Lencioni

In the Realm of Hungry Ghosts: Close Encounters with Addiction by Gabor Maté, MD and Peter A. Levine, PhD

Mindfulness by Ellen J. Langer, PhD

The Obstacle Is the Way: The Timeless Art of Turning Trials into Triumph by Ryan Holiday

On Death and Dying: What the Dying Have to Teach Doctors, Nurses, Clergy and Their Own Families by Elisabeth Kubler-Ross

The Power of the Other: The Startling Effect Other People Have on You, from the Boardroom to the Bedroom and Beyond—and What to Do About It by Henry Cloud, PhD

Scattered: How Attention Deficit Disorder Originates and What You Can Do About It by Gabor Maté, MD

The Slavery of Death by Richard Beck, PhD

Solve for Happy: Engineer Your Path to Joy by Mo Gawdat

Surprised by Hope: Rethinking Heaven, the Resurrection, and the Mission of the Church by N.T. Wright

Thinking, Fast and Slow by Daniel Kahneman

The Total Money Makeover: A Proven Plan for Financial Fitness by Dave Ramsey

Trauma and Recovery: The Aftermath of Violence—From Domestic Abuse to Political Terror by Judith Lewis Herman, MD

Trauma: The Invisible Epidemic: How Trauma Works and How We Can Heal from It by Paul Conti, MD

Trauma Stewardship: An Everyday Guide to Caring for Self While Caring for Others by Laura van Dernoot Lipsky with Connie Burk

The Untethered Soul: The Journey Beyond Yourself by Michael A. Singer

Waking the Tiger: Healing Trauma by Peter A. Levine with Ann Frederick

Why We Sleep: Unlocking the Power of Sleep and Dreams by Matthew Walker, PhD

Why Zebras Don't Get Ulcers by Robert M. Sapolsky

Answering Life's Messy Questions

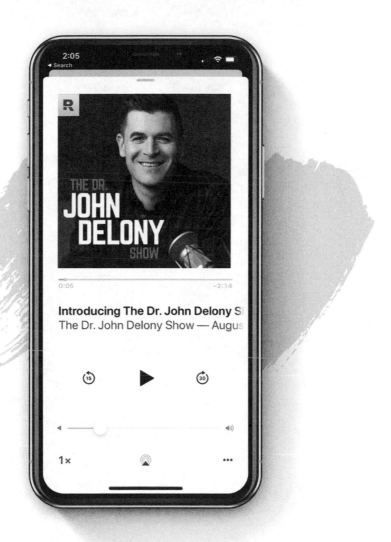

The Dr. John Delony Show is a caller-driven show that helps you find the answers to questions about mental health, wellness, relationships, and more.

ramseysolutions.com/john-delony

Connect

with the people who matter most.

Starting a good conversation can be hard—but it doesn't have to be!
With Dr. John Delony's Questions for Humans Conversation Cards,
you can easily have meaningful (and fun) quality time with your
spouse, kids, and friends.

ramseysolutions.com/store